Forensic Accounting in Matrimonial Divorce

James A. DiGabriele
Editor

Edwards

ISBN: 1-930217-12-9
ISSN 1524-5586

Edwards   www.rtedwards.com

© 2005 R.T. Edwards, Inc. All rights reserved. Neither this work nor any part thereof may be reproduced or transmitted in any form or by any means whatsoever – including photocopying, microfilming, and recording, or by any information storage or retrieval system – without prior written permission from the publisher. For ordering information or reprint permission, please contact: R.T. Edwards, Inc., P.O. Box 27388, Philadelphia, PA 19118 USA.

Information contained in this work has been obtained by R.T. Edwards, Inc. ("R.T. Edwards") from authentic and highly regarded sources believed to be reliable. However, neither R.T. Edwards nor its authors guarantee the accuracy or completeness of any information contained herein, and neither R.T. Edwards nor its authors shall be responsible for errors or omissions, or for the consequences or damages arising out of the use of this information. This work is published with the understanding that R.T. Edwards and its authors are supplying information but are not attempting to render accounting, legal, investment, or other professional services. If such services are required, the assistance of an appropriate professional should be sought.

Library of Congress Cataloging-in-Publication Data

Forensic accounting in matrimonial divorce / edited by James A. DiGabriele.-- 1st ed.
   p. cm.
  Includes bibliographical references and index.
  ISBN 1-930217-12-9 (alk. paper)
   1. Divorce settlements--United States--Accounting. 2. Forensic accounting--United States. 3. Marital property--Valuation--United States. 4. Divorce--Economic aspects--United States. I. DiGabriele, James A., 1962-
   KF535.7.F67 2005
   346.7301'66--dc22
                                             2004021605

   1 2 3 4 5 LS 5 6 7 8 9
Printed in the United States of America

CONTENTS

Preface v

1 The Role of Accountants in Divorce Cases 1
   William J. Morrison and Thomas J. Reck

2 Ethical Limitations on Future Services for Neutral
   Financial Professionals Following a Collaborative
   Divorce 19
   David C. Hesser

3 Complex Compensation Issues in a Divorce 31
   Susan M. Mangiero and Lili A. Vasileff

4 Valuing Professional Practices for Divorce
   Engagements: Reasonable Compensation and
   Excess Earnings – Hit or Myth? 43
   Kevin R. Yeanoplos

5 Unreported Income and Hidden Assets 49
   Mark Kohn

6 Equitable Distribution and Community Property
   States 65
   Joyce C. Somerville

7 Business Owner Investigative Techniques: A Focus
   on Fringe Benefits 71
   James F. McNulty

8	Factors to Consider Regarding Division of Non-Marital and Marital Assets for Divorce	97
	Richard A. Campanella and Joseph M. Lo Campo	
9	Determining Economic Income for Divorce Purposes when the Spouse Owns a Closely Held Business	109
	Bruce L. Richman	
10	Selection of Business Valuation Experts in a Divorce: The Attorney Perspective	133
	Paul Townsend and Alison Leslie	
11	Litigating and Proving Child Support in High Asset or High Income Cases: What to do When a Heavy Hitter is at the Plate	141
	Barry A. Kozyra and Judith A. Hartz	
12	Do Court Preferences Exist in Cases of Matrimonial Dissolution Involving the Valuation of Closely Held Companies?	179
	James A. DiGabriele and Gabriela V. Simoes	
	Contributing Authors	193
	Index	197

PREFACE

Professionals in the field of marital dissolution are often faced with the challenging task of combining financial, accounting, and investigatory expertise together with an understanding of the legal process so as to assist in the disposition of legal matters. This book is intended for such practicing professionals, including, but not limited to, Certified Public Accountants, Certified Divorce Analysts, Divorce Financial Planners, Business Valuation specialists, etc., that are involved in litigation support to provide a factual reporting of economic issues associated with existing, pending or contemplated marital litigation. It is in the interest of all parties that the practitioner be properly equipped to deliver services as efficiently and effectively as possible.

Matrimonial dissolution is highly sensitive and often emotionally charged. While similarities exist, case specific details can vary greatly. A strong functional expertise, an ability to form case-by-case insight, and a general knowledge of the legal framework in which the professional services are demanded and delivered enables the practitioner to maintain a levelheaded and evenhanded perspective while rendering valuable assistance. This book, commissioned as a special supplement to the *Journal of Forensic Accounting,* has been developed to help practitioners in the field of marital dissolution to effectively and efficiently plan and perform their work. To accomplish this, chapters have been selected so as to provide: 1) a contemporary overview of the field; 2) current information on important aspects of marital dissolution; and 3) insights into complexities which may challenge professional awareness and objectivity.

Within the realm of divorce, those factors that have traditionally played a predominant role are often no longer the dominating pieces of the puzzle. "Forensic Accounting in Matrimonial Divorce" attempts to capture the essence of this evolution in both direction and complexity, and focuses upon some of those challenging or recently emergent issues that practitioners must now face on a regular basis. While much of the book concentrates on the basic, though often intricate, notions of identification, allocation, and valuation of dually claimed assets such as businesses, property, and/or other assets. both the breadth and depth of the task at hand calls for the ability to adopt the requisite skepticism and, when circumstances warrant, to act in an investigatory capacity to uncover issues of relevance to client interests. Insight into this attitude of professional skepticism, the resulting suitable level of scrutiny, and the methods of appropriate investigatory approaches, therefore, is another common bond of many of the selected chapters.

This book is intended to be a clear, concise, and informative reference to forensic accounting as a critical component within the process of matrimonial dissolution. In that it is likely that topics covered herein will be central components of some number of important impending engagements, this book is an essential part of every practitioner's library. Moreover, beyond the usefulness of the broad array of relevant topics, it is hoped that this book inspires a mindset which is sharpened to the focus of the realities and passions inherent in matrital dispute engagements..

James A. DiGabriele
West Orange, November 2004

CHAPTER 1

The Role of Accountants in Divorce Cases

William J. Morrison and Thomas J. Reck

INTRODUCTION

Accountants are utilized at the negotiating table and on the witness stand to provide the information needed to negotiate an equitable division of property or to obtain a decision from the court. In this regard, accounting services include the marshalling and evaluation of assets and liabilities subject to equitable distribution. Often, this involves the valuation of closely held businesses and the determination of the true income of the owner spouse. In recent years, the boom in the stock market has caused forensic accountants to focus on the evaluation of the income and assets derived from employee compensation and benefits packages in publicly held corporations, including stock options, phantom stock and the like. Other services that can be performed include pension valuation and the preparation of Qualified Domestic Relations Orders (QDRO).

Much has been written about the above functions, which are primarily those of an expert witness.[1] This paper will focus on the role of an accountant as an economic consultant and resource throughout the divorce case, one who can deliver technical expertise and sound financial judgment. In this regard, the accountant's duties should begin on the day retained. Consequently, you should endeavor to be hired as early in the process as possible - so as to provide maximum value.

---

[1] In addition, the evaluation of stock options, employee benefits and pension plans require special training and knowledge, not possessed by all accountants.

William J. Morrison, CPA/ABV, president of Morrison & Company.
Thomas J. Reck, CPA/ABV, is a partner at Morrison & Company.

The services which accountants typically provide include:
1. Preliminary evaluations
2. Lifestyle analyses
3. Preparation of Case Information Statements
4. Disposable income analyses
5. Tax analyses for alimony, child support and equitable distribution
6. Pendente Lite applications
7. Assistance in discovery and depositions
8. Assistance in negotiations

PRELIMINARY EVALUATIONS

Often, a forensic accountant is called by an attorney and advised that they are in negotiations. If the matter cannot be resolved, they will retain forensic accounting services in order to value the business and determine the business owner's income. This is a very dangerous process. It is equivalent to "Fire – Aim – Ready" instead of "Ready – Aim – Fire" because you are negotiating before you have marshaled the assets and determined the income. This process may work for W-2 wage earners who have few assets. Most divorce cases today, however, also include a house, stock portfolio, pension accounts, and employee benefits where prudence would suggest the early utilization of a forensic accountant.

In order to negotiate, you must understand the assets and liabilities subject to equitable distribution and income available for support. At the very least, the accountant should be allowed to perform sufficient work[2] to reach preliminary conclusions of value, so that even early settlement proposals can be evaluated if the client insists on settling at this juncture.

It is also important to engage the accountant early, so that the client may begin to deal with the actual economic realities. Often, figures may be presented which may be artificially high or low. As a result, clients may have unrealistic expectations. In addition, even if you are not in negotiations, it is helpful to perform a preliminary analysis of the income and the marital estate in order to understand the magnitude of the income, assets and liabilities.

---

[2] We take no position on what is sufficient work.

LIFESTYLE ANALYSES

A lifestyle analysis is prepared in order to:

1. *Determine the lifestyle enjoyed by the parties during the marriage.*
    Based upon New Jersey's statutes, the standard of living enjoyed during the marriage is a factor to be considered in the determination of both alimony and child support. As a result, a lifestyle analysis is extremely important for the preparation of the Case Information Statement (CIS). The analysis provides the necessary information to negotiate or try the issues of alimony and child support.

To determine the lifestyle enjoyed during the marriage, a forensic accountant will:

   Inquire as to how the family paid for their lifestyle
   - Checks (how many accounts)
   - ATM machines / cash (reported and unreported)
   - Credit cards (how many cards)
   - Barter
   - Business perquisites (perks)

Assuming the family lived off a paycheck, that was deposited into one checking account, the lifestyle analysis is very straightforward. In this case, the forensic accountant may input the checkbook and credit card information into a computer using programs customized to analyze the data.

2. *Investigate allegations of cash of unreported income.*
    To investigate unreported income, the forensic accountant will require several years of personal bank account and credit card statements of the parties, including checkbook registers, canceled checks and deposit slips.

Case Information Statements

Accountants can prepare Case Information Statements (CIS) based on the actual spending of the parties. CIS preparation is a subset of the lifestyle analyses discussed above. In essence, the accountant interviews the client and inquires as to how the family lived: through a checkbook, unreported cash, barter, and/or personal payments of expenses by the business (perks). By inputting the family checkbook and credit card statements into the computer, a CIS, which presents the actual lifestyle and needs of the parties, can be prepared.

The forensic accountant will proceed as follows:

- A. Interview the non-working spouse. We ask that they be specific about the details surrounding unreported income and provide corroborative documentation. If it is asserted that the couple lived on more than the reported income, fill out the following:

    i. Lifestyle Questionnaire[3] (Exhibit A-1)

    ii. Hidden Income Questionnaire[3] (Exhibit A-2)

- B. Input bank and credit card information into the computer. Set up categories based upon the line items used on the CIS. (When requested by attorneys we input the results of our analysis into a spreadsheet format that mirrors the format of the CIS.)

- C. Conduct an inspection of the business premises and interview the working spouse.

- D. Perform perquisite analysis based upon the oral interviews and the analytical review of business tax returns.

- E. Draw preliminary conclusions.

- F. Re-interview non-working and working spouse, if warranted based upon preliminary conclusions.

- G. Finalize conclusions; prepare findings.

One way to test this analysis for reasonableness is to compare the Case Information Statements of the two parties to see if they are in agreement. This step may also serve as a proxy for a full lifestyle analysis if the CIS comparison shows the parties to be in general agreement on their lifestyle.

---

[3] These are questionnaires we use to uncover unreported income. All chapter Exhibits may be found following the conclusion to this chapter.

Disposable Income Analyses

Accountants can prepare analyses which calculate the net after-tax income available to each party based upon different levels of alimony and child support and/or different amounts of actual or imputed income. Several computer programs are available to prepare these analyses. Exhibits B1-4 shows the net disposable income available to parties under the following parameters:

- payor spouse earns income between $300,000 and $350,000
- payee spouse earns or has imputed income of $30,000
- alimony between $26,000 and $72,000
- child support at a constant $26,000

As shown in these Exhibits, the net disposable income ranges from $115,030 to $170,028 for the payor spouse and $72,333 to $104,127 for the payee spouse.

Tax Analyses

Probably the most basic service an accountant can provide is an analysis of the tax consequences for different amounts of alimony and different forms of equitable distribution. For example, accountants analyze the tax effects of alimony, pensions, the transfer of assets and equitable distribution. An often-overlooked area is the tax liability associated with a partnership interest. The purpose of this chapter is not to argue hypothetical versus actual tax consequences, but to explain that tax consequences can be calculated and presented by an accountant. Because there are tax consequences to alimony and equitable distribution, these consequences need to be known in order to make informed and reasoned decisions. For example, a pension plan distribution of $100,000 with a 40% effective tax rate due upon distribution is worth $60,000. A savings account of $100,000 with no tax consequence is worth the full $100,000.

Exhibit C shows the Federal Personal Tax Rates for ordinary income.

Pendente Lite Applications

The accountant's determination of the business owner's income, net disposable income and lifestyle analyses are all very helpful to ensure a fair award of support. If the judge awards support on the tax returns, the award may be too low. If he awards it on unsubstantiated allegations of spending, it may be too high. An accountant is best able to fairly represent the parties' income and spending, and is needed to calculate the taxes on any taxable award of support so that the non-earning spouse will have sufficient funds to pay taxes. In fact, one of the biggest issues faced in matrimonial cases is the Pendente Lite award, which does not include a tax factor. Pendente Lite means "pending in litigation" and is used to describe temporary alimony or child support awarded prior to settlement or trial.

Discovery

The role of an accountant in economic discovery cannot be over emphasized. The most critical function of an accountant in discovery is to perform the required accounting, financial, economic and valuation analyses, to determine the extent to which the books and records must be investigated (and consequently, the fees incurred) in order to verify the income available for support and the assets and liabilities subject to equitable distribution. The most costly and time-consuming part of matrimonial cases is the actual work of obtaining information and pouring over records. The accountant should be able to determine which records are needed and the manner in which they need to be analyzed so that he can verify the assets and liabilities subject to equitable distribution and the income available for support.

Sometimes, each check in the checkbook must be analyzed; other times the same result can be obtained by analyzing completed documents, such as financial statements and tax returns. The accountant should advise the client on the timing and extent of the work to be performed, so that the marital estate can be marshaled and sufficient evidence gathered to be presented in court.

Exhibit D is our Divorce Settlement Checklist. Such a checklist is useful to ensure completeness in considering aspects of discovery.

The following statements can create difficult issues:

> "We always lived well, now we have nothing," **OR**,
>
> "The business always made money, but now that we are getting divorced, he says the business is doing poorly."

These statements prompt the use of an accountant. First and foremost, the accountant must be a financial analyst. Second, the accountant needs an understanding of economics in order to advise the client if the business downturn is caused by economic factors beyond the owner's control, or if on a preliminary review, he believes the owner is underreporting income and/or hiding assets.

Depositions

In depositions, accountants can provide questions and guidance on economic matters. In fact, it is very dangerous to take a deposition on economic matters without the assistance of a forensic accountant.

Negotiations

An accountant is a valuable tool in negotiations because he can:

1. Analyze the other side's position and determine if the position is reasonable in light of the overall assets, liabilities, income, liquidity, and tax consequences.
2. Help in preparation of the client position.
3. Help prepare creative solutions using tax consequences, liquidity, and the value of money to structure a settlement.

CONCLUSION

When properly utilized, a forensic accountant becomes a valuable consultant throughout a divorce case. They can provide technical assistance, as well as guidance and judgment on financial matters at every phase of the case.

APPENDIX: THE ROLE OF ACCOUTANTS IN DIVORCE CASES

Exhibit A-1   LIFESTYLE QUESTIONNAIRE

1. Are the estimated personal living expenses reported on the C.I.S. reflective of the family's standard of living during the marriage?

2. Do they include taxes?

3. How many vehicles are driven by the family (describe vehicle and person who drives it)?

4. Has the couple entertained much in the last three years (if yes, describe the types of entertaining)?

5. What business or personal trips have either or both spouses taken during the last three years (describe trip and parties involved)?

6. Where does the family vacation? How often?

7. During the last three years, what amount of purchases were for furs, jewelry, art work, or collectibles (indicate amount and description of items purchased)?

8. How many times a week and in what restaurants do either or both spouses dine out?

9. What other luxuries has the family enjoyed during the last three years (indicate type and cost of luxury and the source of funds used to pay for the luxuries)?

10. Describe the manner in which salaries are paid. For example, did you receive a check or were personal expenditures paid by the company and

charged to you as salary? Does your compensation include phantom income or loans? (Phantom income is reported income without actual cash payments.)

Source of Funds for Lifestyle:

11. How were the above expenses paid for? Business (perquisites), personal check, credit card, barter, borrowings, business or personal assets, or cash?

12. If business perks received, were they reported as income?

13. Which expenses were paid directly by personal check and which by credit card?

14. Describe any barter arrangements including the value of the services received and the frequency.

15. If you have lived on borrowings or the failure to pay expenses, describe. Business (type); Personal (type); failure to pay trade creditors or the government.

16. If you lived on the sale of business or personal assets, describe the assets liquidated. Was this before or after the complaint for divorce was filed?

17. What funds were received in the form of loans, gifts, or inheritances (indicate amounts and dates received)?

18. What fringe benefits helped maintain the family's standard of living (indicate approximate annual amounts)?

19. What income is received by the lower earning spouse and/or children that is used to help support the family's standard of living (indicate amounts)?

Exhibit A-2 HIDDEN INCOME QUESTIONNAIRE

Were any of the expenditures paid with unreported cash? Unreported cash or hidden income that should be available for support of the family but whose existence has not been disclosed. In and of itself, the payment of expenditures in cash may not be an indication of unreported income. Cash may be derived from bank withdrawals; writing checks to cash; cashing paychecks; depositing a portion of a paycheck and taking the remainder in cash and many other legitimate means.

1. What income is received that is not reported on the personal income tax returns (indicate amounts)?

2. Do you have knowledge of any hidden income?
   __ If yes, continue with the questions in this section. *If no, go to question 6.*

3. What is the basis of your knowledge, and what documents support that knowledge?

4. What is the source of hidden or deferred income, who received it, and what methods were used to hide or defer it?

5. What amount of hidden income is received each week, and how much is received in cash?

6. Where is the hidden income kept (bank account, brokerage firm, safety deposit box, etc.), and what is it primarily used for?

Changes in Lifestyle:

7. Has your lifestyle changed since the contemplation of divorce or the start of the divorce action?

8. Has your business changed? Have either the revenues or expenses changed?

Hidden or transferred property:
Hidden property is property that belongs to the marital estate and whose existence has not been disclosed to the client. Transferred property is property that would have been available for use by the marital estate if it had not been transferred to someone else.

9. Do you have knowledge of any hidden or transferred property?
   __ If yes, continue with the questions in this section.

10. What is the basis of your knowledge, and what documents support that knowledge?
   _____
   _____

11. In whose name is the property titled?
   _____
   _____

12. What amount of consideration was received for the transferred property?
   _____
   _____

13. How was the property acquired?
   _____
   _____

Exhibit B-1   Net Disposable Income Analysis

	Gross Income of payer spouse:	$300,000
	Alimony:	$ 26,000

Sample
Wednesday, July 14, 2004

	Payor	Recipient
Name	John Smith	Jane Smith
Filing Status	Single	Head of Household
Exemptions	1	2
State	NJ	NJ
Pre-set Alimony		26000
Pre-set Child Support		26000
Computed Disposable Net	141701	72333
Income & Adjustments:		
Gross Income	300000	30000
Alimony (Income Adjustment)	-26000	26000
Other Income Adjustments	0	0
Non-taxable Income	0	0
Adjusted Gross Income	274000	56000
Itemized/Standard Deductions	-4750	-7000
Phased-off Exemptions	0	-6100
Federal Taxable Income	269250	42900
State Additions to Income	0	0
State Subtractions from Income	0	0
State Exemptions	1000	4000
State Taxable Inc	273000	52000
Income-taxes:		
Federal Taxes	81290	6518
State Taxes	15265	854
City/Local Taxes	0	0
FICA/OASDI/Medicare	9744	2295
Federal Credits	0	0
Total Taxes	106299	9667
After-tax Summary:		
Gross Income	300000	30000
Total Taxes	-106299	-9667
Alimony	-26000	26000
Child Support	-26000	26000
Mandatory Adjustments	0	0
Disposable Net Income	141701	72333
Marginal Federal Tax Rate	0.35	0.27
Marginal State Tax Rate	0.0637	0.0245

Exhibit B-2 Net Disposable Income Analysis

Gross Income of payer spouse: $300,000
Alimony: $ 72,000

Sample
Wednesday, July 14, 2004

	Payor	Recipient
Name	John Smith	Jane Smith
Filing Status	Single	Head of Household
Exemptions	1	2
State	NJ	NJ
Pre-set Alimony		72000
Pre-set Child Support		26000
Computed Disposable Net	115030	104127
Income & Adjustments:		
Gross Income	300000	30000
Alimony (Income Adjustment)	-72000	72000
Other Income Adjustments	0	0
Non-taxable Income	0	0
Adjusted Gross Income	228000	102000
Itemized/Standard Deductions	-4750	-7000
Phased-off Exemptions	-854	-6100
Federal Taxable Income	222396	88900
State Additions to Income	0	0
State Subtractions from Income	0	0
State Exemptions	1000	4000
State Taxable Inc	227000	98000
Income-taxes:		
Federal Taxes	64892	18938
State Taxes	12334	2640
City/Local Taxes	0	0
FICA/OASDI/Medicare	9744	2295
Federal Credits	0	0
Total Taxes	86970	23873
After-tax Summary:		
Gross Income	300000	30000
Total Taxes	-86970	-23873
Alimony	-72000	72000
Child_Support	-26000	26000
Mandatory Adjustments	0	0
Disposable Net Income	115030	104127
Marginal Federal Tax Rate	0.35	0.27
Marginal State Tax Rate	0.0637	0.05525

Exhibit B-3   Net Disposable Income Analysis

	Gross Income of payer spouse:	$350,000
	Alimony:	$ 26,000

Sample
Wednesday, July 14, 2004

	Payor	Recipient
Name	John Smith	Jane Smith
Filing Status	Single	Head of Household
Exemptions	1	2
State	NJ	NJ
Pre-set Alimony		26000
Pre-set Child Support		26000
Computed Disposable Net	170028	72333
Income & Adjustments:		
Gross Income	350000	30000
Alimony (Income Adjustment)	-26000	26000
Other Income Adjustments	0	0
Non-taxable Income	0	0
Adjusted Gross Income	324000	56000
Itemized/Standard Deductions	-4750	-7000
Phased-off Exemptions	0	-6100
Federal Taxable Income	319250	42900
State Additions to Income	0	0
State Subtractions from Income	0	0
State Exemptions	1000	4000
State Taxable Inc	323000	52000
Income-taxes:		
Federal Taxes	99053	6518
State Taxes	18450	854
City/Local Taxes	0	0
FICA/OASDI/Medicare	10469	2295
Federal Credits	0	0
Total Taxes	127972	9667
After-tax Summary:		
Gross Income	350000	30000
Total Taxes	-127972	-9667
Alimony	-26000	26000
Child_Support	-26000	26000
Mandatory Adjustments	0	0
Disposable Net Income	170028	72333
Marginal Federal Tax Rate	0.386	0.27
Marginal State Tax Rate	0.0637	0.0245

The Role of Accountants in Divorce Cases

Exhibit B-4   Net Disposable Income Analysis

Gross Income of payer spouse: $350,000
Alimony: $ 72,000

Sample
Wednesday, July 14, 2004

	Payor	Recipient
Name	John Smith	Jane Smith
Filing Status	Single	Head of Household
Exemptions	1	2
State	NJ	NJ
Pre-set Alimony		72000
Pre-set Child Support		26000
Computed Disposable Net	143322	104127
Income & Adjustments:		
Gross Income	350000	30000
Alimony (Income Adjustment)	-72000	72000
Other Income Adjustments	0	0
Non-taxable Income	0	0
Adjusted Gross Income	278000	102000
Itemized/Standard Deductions	-4750	-7000
Phased-off Exemptions	0	-6100
Federal Taxable Income	273250	88900
State Additions to Income	0	0
State Subtractions from Income	0	0
State Exemptions	1000	4000
State Taxable Inc	277000	98000
Income-taxes:		
Federal Taxes	82690	18938
State Taxes	15519	2640
City/Local Taxes	0	0
FICA/OASDI/Medicare	10469	2295
Federal Credits	0	0
Total Taxes	108678	23873
After-tax Summary:		
Gross Income	350000	30000
Total Taxes	-108678	-23873
Alimony	-72000	72000
Child_Support	-26000	26000
Mandatory Adjustments	0	0
Disposable Net Income	143322	104127
Marginal Federal Tax Rate	0.35	0.27
Marginal State Tax Rate	0.0637	0.05525

Exhibit C   2004 and 2005 Federal Personal Tax Rates

2004 Ordinary Taxable Income

Marginal Tax Rate	Single Filers	Married Filing Jointly / Surviving Spouse	Married Filing Separately	Head of Household
10%	0 - 7,150	0 - 14,300	0 - 7,150	0 - 10,200
15%	7,151 - 29,050	14,301 - 58,100	7,151 - 29,050	10,201 - 38,900
25%	29,051 - 70,350	58,101 - 117,250	29,051 - 58,625	38,901 - 100,500
28%	70,351 - 46,750	117,251 - 178,650	58,626 - 89,325	100,501 - 162,700
33%	146,751 - 319,100	178,651 - 319,100	89,326 - 159,550	162,701 - 319,100
45%	319,101 or more	319,101 or more	159,551 or more	319,101 or more

2005 Ordinary Taxable Income (Projected*)

Marginal Tax Rate	Single Filers	Married Filing Jointly / Surviving Spouse	Married Filing Separately	Head of Household
10%	0 - 7,300	0 - 14,600	0 - 7,300	0 - 10,450
15%	7,301 - 29,700	14,601 - 59,400	7,301 - 29,700	10,451 - 39,800
25%	29,701 - 71,950	59,401 - 119,950	29,701 - 59,975	39,801 - 102,800
28%	71,951 - 150,150	119,951 - 182,800	59,976 - 91,400	102,801 - 166,450
33%	150,151 - 326,450	182,801 - 326,450	91,401 - 163,225	166,451 - 326,450
45%	326,451 or more	326,451 or more	163,226 or more	326,451 or more

*Projections by CCH Incorporated per September 22, 2004 press release, based on various indexing and legislative assumptions. These projections are provided for illustrative purposes only and are not to be relied upon. Only the Internal Revenue Service provides official rate and bracket information.

Exhibit D   Preliminary Discovery Checklist

DIVORCE SETTLEMENT CHECKLIST

INCOME
- ☐ COLA
  Cost of living adjustment for alimony or child support
- ☐ Alimony
  Term/Recapture
  Non-taxable v. taxable
  Step down
- ☐ Child support
- ☐ Income tax refunds
  Allocation
  Payments due
  Refunds

EXPENSES
- ☐ Medical/dental insurance
  Spouse
  Children
- ☐ Un-reimbursed (medical/dental)
- ☐ Life insurance
  (alimony, child support)
- ☐ Tuition (private school)
- ☐ Child costs
  Child care, camp
  After school, lessons
- ☐ College
- ☐ Special needs children
- ☐ Relocation

TAX CONSEQUENCES
- ☐ Business
- ☐ Real estate
- ☐ Stock/pension
- ☐ Marital residence
- ☐ Pendente lite support
- ☐ Basis of items transferred
- ☐ Filing status
- ☐ Deferred taxes
- ☐ Exemptions (children)
- ☐ Estimated tax payments

- ☐ Innocent spouse provision
- ☐ Indemnification

ASSETS
- ☐ Accrued interest/market changes to date of payment
  Pension/retirement accounts
  Bank/investment accounts
  Deferred compensation plans
- ☐ Miscellaneous assets
  Personal Property
  Cars
  Frequent flyer miles
  Security deposits
  Passive activity loss carry forward
  Capital loss carry forward
  Investment interest carry forward
- ☐ Tangible property
  Appraisal v. in-kind swap
  Jewelry/fine arts/collections

LIABILITIES
- ☐ Counsel and expert fees
- ☐ Mortgage releases
- ☐ Miscellaneous liabilities
  Credit cards
  Family loans
- ☐ Indemnification

OTHER
- ☐ Lepis/anti-lepis provision
- ☐ Parenting schedule
- ☐ Changes circumstances
  (triggering events status)
- ☐ Will revisions
- ☐ Change of beneficiary
  Retirement accounts
  Life insurance
- ☐ Deed transfer on real estate
- ☐ Payment of arrearages
- ☐ Crews analysis (lifestyle)

DIVORCE SETTLEMENT CHECKLIST
EQUITABLE DISTRIBUTION FACTORS

Pursuant to N.J.S.A. 2A:34-23, these are the factors to be considered by the Court in determining equitable distribution. They are similar to the factors to be considered for alimony and child support.

☐ The duration of the marriage

☐ The age and physical and emotional health of the parties

☐ The income or property brought to the marriage by each party

☐ The standard of living established during the marriage

☐ Any written agreement made by the parties before or during the marriage concerning an arrangement of property distribution

☐ The economic circumstances of each party at the time the division of property becomes effective

☐ The income and earning capacity of each party including educational background, training, employment skills, work experience, length of absence from the job market, custodial responsibilities for children, and the time and expense necessary to acquire sufficient education or training to enable the party to become self-supporting at a standard of living reasonably comparable to that enjoyed during the marriage

☐ The contribution by each party to the education, training or earning power of the other

☐ The contribution of each party to the acquisition, dissipation, preservation, depreciation or appreciation in the amount or value of the martial property as well as the contribution of a party as a homemaker

☐ The tax consequences of the proposed distribution to each party

☐ The present value of the property

☐ The need of a parent who has physical custody of a child to won or occupy the martial residence and t o use or won the household effects

☐ The debts and liabilities of the parties

☐ The need for creation, now or in the future, of a trust fund to secure reasonably foreseeable medical or educational costs for a spouse or children

☐ Any other factors that the court may deem relevant.

CHAPTER 2

Ethical Limitations on Future Services for Neutral Financial Professionals Following a Collaborative Divorce

David C. Hesser

INTRODUCTION

Upon the enactment of "no-fault" divorce, the death knell rang to the institution of marriage. The general public was led to believe that a no-fault divorce would include a minimum of animosity between divorcing parties through relief of proof of fault, a lessening of expense via an abbreviated litigation process, and a granting of a final divorce within six months to a year. Discontented partners ran to seek counsel to secure a speedy and "cheap" divorce. Unfortunately, the fall-out from hasty divorces included numerous unresolved emotional and financial issues, which affected not only the spouses, but also the children, who were traumatized by the dissolution of their family home and by unmet financial needs. Shannon Demick explained a child's emotional problems arising from divorce as follows:

> There is much controversy about how divorce affects children. Many studies show that, **to a child, divorce is equivalent to the pain of the death of the parent.** There is a great loss, with grief and sadness, and confusion for the children. Children most always believe that they are the cause of the divorce. They think that the parent who left, actually left them or left because of them and that the parent doesn't love them anymore. Often the parents

---

David C. Hesser is an Attorney at Law and Certified Divorce Financial Analyst at Gold, Weems, Bruser, Sues & Rundell in Alexandria, Louisiana.

are so consumed in their own grief or turmoil that they fail to see the devastating effects of the breakup on the children.[2]

In addition to the severe emotional problems caused by divorce, the process can financially ruin many divorcees. In many cases former spouses lose retirement benefits,[3] fail to secure much needed alimony, are never paid child support, or the community assets are divided with no consideration of the tax consequences.

Although the judicial system managed to resolve tens of thousands of divorces, the vast number of cases clogged the system and further damaged family relationships.[4] To remedy this, some jurisdictions created family law courts. These specialized courts improved the situation, but they did not address the source of the problem. The courts employed hearing officers and magistrate judges for divorce cases, but this only shifted the problem to someone else instead of addressing the source of the problem. Family law attorneys in the United States adopted mediation as a method to resolve divorce cases, but the method was also not fully equipped to handle divorces.[5] Each method to handle divorces failed because it did not have the proper components to address the unique issues of divorce: finance, emotion and law.[6] Collaborative divorce is the only method of resolving divorces that is fully equipped to address all three components of divorce.[7]

---

[2] Shannon Demick, Divorce and How it Affects a Child (2002), at http://nh.essortment.com/divorcehoweffe_rhcq.htm. [Emphasis added].

[3] See generally, *Stahl v. Exxon Corp.*, 212 F. Supp. 2d 657 (S.D. Tex. 2002), where a former wife lost retirement benefits for failure to obtain a qualified domestic relations order before her ex-husband's death.

[4] Some courts spent seventy-five percent of the court's time on divorce cases even though the cases only accounted for twenty-five percent of the docket load. Interview with Ross Foote, Judge Ninth Judicial District Court Rapides Parish Louisiana, in Toronto, Canada (Sept. 23, 2003), at http://www.collaborativefamilylawassociation.com/.

[5] "Mediation is often inadequate . . . due to mediators' difficulties in managing power imbalances and emotional dynamics of the parties." Pauline H. Tesler, *Collaborative Law: Achieving Effective Resolution In Divorce Without Litigation* 3, 9, 224-25 (2001).

[6] In the 1970s mental health experts began to recognize that divorce was more than just a legal process but was a combination of legal and psychological matters. Jay Folberg & Ann Milne, *Divorce Mediation, Theory And Practice* 3, 5 (Guilford Press 1998).

[7] John Lande has commented that the collaborative law "movement could produce a major advance in dispute resolution. . . ." John Lande, "Possibilities for Collaborative Law: Ethics and Practice of Lawyer Disqualification and Process Control in a New Model of Lawyering" 64 *Ohio St. L. J.* 1315, 1330 (2003).

THE COLLABORATIVE DIVORCE PROCESS [8]

Collaborative divorce is a relatively new method of obtaining a divorce, wherein the couple is assisted by attorneys, mental health coaches, a neutral child specialist, and a neutral financial professional (NFP).[9] The process requires training for all of the professionals where they learn to emphasize honesty, cooperation, integrity and respect.[10] This process helps the couple and the children to begin rebuilding their lives without submitting their dispute for a decision by the court.[11] Collaborative divorce is the first alternative dispute resolution method that provides neutral professionals to assess the couples' financial needs and the childrens' needs.

When a couple decides to submit their dispute to collaborative divorce, they sign an agreement that they will not seek a judicial determination of their divorce issues.[12] They attach the agreement to a collaborative divorce petition, which is filed with the court. The initial filing includes orders to prevent either party from disposing of the couple's assets and specifies who is going to use certain assets while the couple is completing the process. After the initial agreement is signed each spouse selects a mental health coach. The spouses meet individually with their coaches and meet in four-way meetings with the coaches. The coaches' role is not that of a therapist, but seeks to identify problem issues and help the couple prepare to negotiate a settlement.[13] When the mental health coaches have identified the problem issues, they communicate this information to the attorneys, who meet with the spouses in four-way settlement meetings.[14]

Each party has its own attorney, which is an improvement over mediation, where each side may not have an attorney to give legal advice. The four-

---

[8] This article concerns the multi-disciplinary collaborative divorce model that evolved from the original attorney-driven model. See generally, Tesler, supra note 5, at 26 n. 9.

[9] Pauline H. Tesler et al., *Collaborative Divorce Training*, § Introduction 4 (Mar. 2004) (training manual on file with Loyola University New Orleans School of Law).

[10] Bruce L. Richman, *Guide To Taxes And Financial Issues In Divorce*, 49 (John Wiley & Sons, Inc. 2002); Lande, supra note 7, at 1318, 1321.

[11] Lande, supra note 7, at 1318.

[12] James K. Lawrence, *Collaborative Lawyering: A New Development in Conflict Resolution*, 17 Ohio St. J on Disp. Resol. 431 (2002).

[13] Tesler, supra note 9 § Mental Health 5.

[14] Lande, supra note 7, at 1320.

way meetings with the attorneys differ from a normal settlement conference. The attorneys are trained to discuss the issues in a non-adversarial manner that helps the couple to open up and discuss the issues. The meetings allow the couple to openly share information and documents[15] without fear that the documents will be used in court. The sharing of information and the increased communication during the process increases the chance that the couple will reconcile. All discussions during the process are confidential and cannot be used if either spouse decides to go to court. However, once information is known to both spouses, they could seek to obtain the information through regular discovery methods should the collaborative process break down and one party decide to go to court and litigate. There is a financial incentive for the couple and professionals to make the process work.[16] If in fact the process does break down, the couple will have to hire new attorneys, new mental health professionals and a new NFP. If this happens, the collaborative divorce professionals cannot be called as witnesses.

The evaluation by the neutral child specialist and the NFP often helps the couple to resolve critical issues. The child specialist is better able to convey the children's interest, needs, and co-parenting issues to the parties than an expert hired by one spouse. The same is true for NFPs, who show the parties what it will take to operate two households on the same income, along with different scenarios for dividing the assets.

When the process began in 1990,[17] two attorneys would agree not to go to court and would attempt to resolve the case through four-way meetings with the clients. The other professionals were not necessarily an integral part of the process. This attorney driven model evolved into a multi-disciplinary model where all the professionals were trained at one time. The advantage of this process is that each professional involved is doing what that professional does best. The attorneys focus on legal areas, the mental health coaches and child specialist focus on mental areas, and the NFP focuses on financial areas. This lets each discipline do their job and work together for a solution. The multi-disciplinary model has been implemented in the United States and Canada with much success.

---

[15] Richman, supra note 10, at 50.

[16] Id.

[17] Tesler, supra note 5, at xix; Sheila M. Gutterman, "Collaborative Family Law-Part I", 30 *Colo Law.*, Nov. 57 (2001).

The addition of NFPs to the team of professionals added a new and important role for financial professionals. Financial professionals, such as CPAs and Certified Financial Planners, have been offering services to divorcing couples for many years. More recently, the Institute for Divorce Financial Analysts (IDFA) became the leading provider of divorce training for financial professionals. Initially, the IDFA's training was designed to enable the professional to testify as an expert in divorce cases. The training provides the necessary skills for the financial professional to serve the financial needs of a divorcing couple and when combined with collaborative divorce training, the financial professional is ideally suited to be a NFP. As collaborative divorce gains widespread acceptance, it is expected that the financial professional will continue to play a vital role.

QUALIFICATIONS FOR NEUTRAL FINANCIAL PROFESSIONALS

At Loyola University New Orleans Law School's collaborative divorce training seminar in March 2004, the training team included distinguished International Academy of Collaborative Professionals (IACP) officers and directors, Pauline Tesler, Peggy Thompson and Nancy Ross.[18] The training team indicated that NFPs should complete the collaborative divorce training and have the following qualifications:

A. Preferably trained as a Certified Financial Planner (CFP), Chartered Financial Consultant (ChFC), or CPA, possessing a professional license/certification in good standing.

B. Preferably trained as a Certified Divorce Financial Analyst (CDFA), possessing a professional license/certification in good standing.[19]

These are the suggested qualifications and have not been formally adopted as a rule by the IACP or enacted into law. Currently, the local groups who have been trained by IACP members have been implementing internal group rules that generally follow these guidelines. In the future it is expected that each state will enact some rule of law establishing minimum qualifications for NFPs performing collaborative divorce services.

---

[18] These IACP officers and directors conduct many collaborative divorce trainings throughout the United States and Canada and have been instrumental in the rise of collaborative divorce.

[19] Tesler, supra note 9, § Mental Health 48.

THE ROLE OF NEUTRAL FINANCIAL PROFESSIONALS

NFPs provide many valuable services for couples going through a collaborative divorce, including: (1) evaluation of assets and liabilities related to a division of property, (2) evaluation of tax consequences for the division of assets and liabilities, (3) evaluation of alimony issues, (4) evaluation of child support issues, and (5) assistance in creating budgets for two households. These services are performed as a neutral, while considering all the possibilities that would serve both spouses.

NFPs obtain objective information while guarding against favoring one side[20] and should not suggest division of asset scenarios until all the information is available.[21] The couple according to the collaborative divorce agreement agrees to voluntarily produce all relevant information to the NFP.[22] After an NFP gathers all of the information, the NFP should try to educate the couple on the different options[23] without suggesting which options are better.[24] To achieve this, the NFP should inform both spouses about the whole financial picture, using separate meetings with the less informed spouse if needed. [25]

By having NFPs perform financial services, collaborative divorce offers an improvement over traditional divorce. In most divorce cases, the parties do not hire financial experts. Financial experts are usually hired only when there is a significant amount of marital assets involved. In such cases, the spouses hire two experts; as compared to a collaborative divorce where a single NFP is hired, thus costing less and thereby encouraging divorcing couples to obtain much needed financial advice.

---

[20] Mark Hill, *Collaborative Divorce Training*, Collaborative Professional Group of Louisiana (Dec. 10, 2003).
[21] Id.
[22] Id.
[23] Id.
[24] Natalie Leininger, "The Paradigm Shift: A Financial Specialist's Perspective", *Collaborative Rev.*, Fall 2003, at 97.
[25] Hill, supra note 20.

PROPOSED PERMANENT RESTRICTIONS FOR NEUTRAL FINANCIAL PROFESSIONALS

The IACP is an organization founded to promote collaborative divorce.[26] The organization is composed of attorneys, judges, mental health professionals, and financial professionals. The IACP facilitates the necessary training for all the professionals involved in the process including NFPs. In order for the collaborative divorce process to work effectively, board members of the IACP have suggested that collaborative divorce groups establish restrictions on NFPs.[27] In the standard collaborative divorce training materials, the leading trainers, who are IACP board members, recommend that local collaborative groups prohibit NFPs from ever selling any products, investing, or performing other services for either spouse, unless such services are related to the collaborative divorce.[28] The restriction attempts to prevent any appearance of impartiality. The question is whether selling products, investing or providing other services for one of the spouses following a divorce will impair the collaborative process?

Initially, it was thought that NFPs could sell the couple investment products such as life insurance, annuities and mutual funds.[29] The collaborative groups decided that this would create a conflict, since the recommendations of NFPs might become partial to the party who would use the NFP for future investments. Without the sale of any products, NFPs must charge a fee for collaborative divorce services.[30] Some financial companies prohibit their employees from charging a fee for financial services, while others have no restrictions prohibiting fees for services. The difficulty develops when NFPs want to have future client relationships with the divorcees.

---

[26] See IACP's mission statement, at http://www.collabgroup.com/.

[27] The IACP website describes their efforts to establish standards as follows:

A major initiative this year is the development of standards for collaborative practitioners, trainers, and trainings. . . . We also are working on Standards for Practitioners (lawyers, mental health professionals, and financial professionals, whether working in an interdisciplinary team model or not); these draft standards should be ready for circulation to the membership soon.

See the IACP website, at http://www.collabgroup.com/.

[28] Tesler, supra note 9, § Financial 4.

[29] Hill, supra note 20.

[30] Tesler, supra note 9, § Financial 4.

PROBLEMS FOR NEUTRAL FINANCIAL PROFESSIONALS

The proposed restriction that NFPs never perform any post settlement services for the couple could pose a problem for professionals that are not allowed to charge fees for services and for professionals not wanting to restrict their client base. Many professionals interested in working as NFPs have prior experience as experts in divorce cases. The goal of these professionals is to increase their client base for economic gain. If NFPs are not allowed future roles with either spouse, the professional's client base could decrease over time. If the professional had a business relationship with the couple prior to the collaborative divorce case, such as preparing their taxes or selling mutual funds, the professional would not want to handle the collaborative divorce and lose both spouses as clients.

In small metropolitan areas there will be a limited number of financial professionals who complete the collaborative divorce training. The fact that NFPs will be prohibited from doing any work will discourage them from accepting cases. If NFPs accept collaborative divorce cases for wealthy individuals in small metropolitan areas they could substantially reduce their practice. Strangely enough, NFPs would be better served to provide services to less affluent people who have less need for other financial services, than wealthy people who may need future services.

The ethical rules for Certified Public Accountants (CPA) as adopted by the American Institute of Certified Public Accountants (AICPA) do not prohibit CPAs who served as NFPs from providing future services to one of the divorcees. The AICPA rules are not the law in a state unless such rules were adopted by the state.[31] AICPA Rule 03 102-2 explains that a conflict of interest:

> [M]ay occur if a member performs a professional service for a client or employer and the member or his or her firm has a relationship with another person, entity, product, or service that could, in the member's professional judgment, be viewed by the client, employer, or other appropriate parties as impairing the member's objectivity. If the member believes that the professional service can be performed with objectivity, and the relationship

---

[31] A comprehensive evaluation of the CPA ethical rules is beyond the scope of this article.

is disclosed to and consent is obtained from such client, employer, or other appropriate parties, the rule shall not operate to prohibit the performance of the professional service.[32]

The AICPA rule also provides an example of a divorce situation, which may impair the CPA's objectivity.[33]

AICPA Rule 3 102-2 does not prohibit CPAs who served as NFPs from later working for one of the parties. A fair reading of the rule suggests that after a CPA has worked for both spouses incidental to a divorce, that he/she cannot perform future services, which are adverse to the other spouse. This situation could impair the CPA's objectivity and in such a case, the conflict should be disclosed and consent obtained from the client before proceeding with services. Rule 3 102-2 is not clear as to whether CPAs need to disclose and obtain consent from both spouses. Certainly it is the better practice for CPAs to disclose the conflict and obtain both spouses consent before proceeding.

Certified Financial Planners (CFP) are required to follow the CFP Board of Standards Code of Ethics and Professional Responsibility (CFP Code of Ethics). The CFP Code of Ethics Rules 401, 402 and Principle 4 require the disclosure of conflicts of interest.[34] Rule 202 of the CFP Code of Ethics requires CFPs to act in the interest of the client.[35]

The AICPA and the CFP Code of Ethics are somewhat generalized. Neither set of rules prohibits NFPs from providing future services. It is likely that neither organization was specifically contemplating the situation of NFPs when they developed the rules. However, it cannot be ignored that the generalized nature of the rules are designed to encourage employment when there is no real conflict of interest in representing a client. In the case of NFPs performing future work for a divorcee, there may be no real conflict, if the interests of the client are not adverse to the former spouse.

---

[32] American Institute of Certified Public Accountants Rule 03 102-2 (2004), at http://www.aicpa.org/about/code/et102.htm#2.

[33] See comment following AICPA Rule 03 102-2.

[34] Certified Financial Planner Board of Standards Code of Ethics and Professional Responsibility Rules 401, 402, Principle 4 (Rev. 07/2003), http://www.cfp.net/learn/ethics.asp.

[35] Certified Financial Planner Board of Standards Code of Ethics and Professional Responsibility Rule 202 (Rev. 07/2003), at http://www.cfp.net/learn/ethics.asp.

This interpretation of the AICPA and CFP rules is consistent with the ethical rules regulating attorneys, which only prohibit representation of a client when such representation is materially adverse to a former client.[36] Attorneys are allowed to represent clients whose interests are not materially adverse to former clients because such representation promotes employment of attorneys. For the same reason, more financial professionals will be willing to be NFPs if they are not prohibited from providing services under the ethical rules in cases where there is no real conflict.

The IDFA Code of Ethics and Professional Responsibility requires objectivity and fairness for Certified Divorce Financial Analyst (CDFA).[37] The objectivity rule requires CDFAs to be intellectually honest and impartial regardless of which party the CDFA represents.[38] The fairness rule requires that CDFAs maintain independence between the CDFA's financial practice and the divorce practice.[39] While the CDFA rules are generalized in much the same way as the CFP rules, the CDFA rules recognize the potential for problems when combining financial services and divorce services. Currently, the IDFA has not provided any indication of how the fairness rule will be interpreted. To promote the use of a NFP in collaborative divorces, the IDFA should interpret the fairness rule to allow CDFAs to perform financial services for divorcees as long as: The CDFA is not acting as an NFP at the same time he/she provides financial services, and the CDFA who served as an NFP does not provide financial services that are materially adverse to the former spouse.

THE PROPOSED LIMITATIONS

Following a collaborative divorce, NFPs should be allowed to provide future services unrelated to the divorce. This is clear because once a financial settlement is complete, there is little likelihood that the couple will need further divorce related neutral financial services. A couple would only want further neutral financial services if they were going to keep property together following a divorce. Such a practice is almost always

---

[36] "Model rule of professional conduct" Rule 1.9 (2004), http://www.abanet.org/cpr/mrpc/rule_1_9.html.

[37] Institute for Divorce Financial Analysts, Code of Ethics and Professional Responsibility Rules 3, 4 (2004), at https://www.institutedfa.com.

[38] Id. at Rule 3.

[39] Id. at Rule 4.

not recommended due to the long term problems that can arise. Thus, since there is no need for future neutral financial services, NFPs should be allowed to provide future services unrelated to the divorce.

The simplest solution seems to be a limited time restriction before NFPs can represent a former party to a collaborative divorce. This prevents NFPs from making settlement suggestions where they might later invest the funds. A two-year limit on NFPs performing services following the date of the property settlement would be long enough to achieve this result. Few people would wait two-years after their divorce before investing funds from the divorce. Such a limit maintains impartiality for the financial neutrals and encourages their participation in the collaborative divorce process in both large cities and small metropolitan areas.

The role of NFPs and the suggested limitations should be distinguished from the role of mediators whose role and interest are different from NFPs. Neutral mediators are prohibited from future representation of former clients to divorce mediation, unless informed consent is obtained.[40] Mediators differ from financial professionals, because mediators devote the majority of their practice to mediation and may not need to accept other non-mediation business. It is expected that NFPs will not be dedicating the majority of their practice to collaborative divorce. Even if mediators are not distinguished from NFPs, the ABA Rule allows future representation of past mediation clients, when informed consent is obtained. The only difference between the suggested limitations for NFPs and the ethical limitations for mediators is that mediators must obtain informed consent whereas NFPs need only wait the two-year period.

Should the two-year limitation be reduced if the other spouse consents in writing? In order to maintain neutrality and to avoid a spouse being pressured by a dominating former spouse, there should be a minimum limitation of one-year before NFPs can represent divorcees even when written consent is obtained. A one-year restriction with written consent maintains impartiality and promotes the use of NFPs in collaborative divorce without jeopardizing the collaborative divorce process.

Should NFPs be allowed to refer divorcees to other financial professionals who are partners or members of the same firm? This question also raises

---

[40] "Model rule of professional conduct" Rule 1.12 (2004), http://www.abanet.org/cpr/mrpc/rule_1_12.html.

the issue of impartiality. If such a practice is allowed, without the two-year/one-year limitation with written consent, it could cause NFPs to be partial and such practice should not be allowed. This issue shows the importance of reasonable limitations. Unreasonable restrictions could encourage NFPs to refer the divorcee to other financial professionals and obtain a referral fee.

In order for the suggested solutions to maintain impartiality of NFPs, they must never take a materially adverse position to the non-client spouse without consent of that spouse. This requirement is similar to the duty of loyalty which attorneys owe their clients. An attorney is not allowed to represent a client whose interest is materially adverse to a former client unless a waiver of conflict form is signed by the former client.[41]

CONCLUSION

The two-year/one-year limitation with waiver prevents impartiality by NFPs and encourages financial processionals to serve as neutrals. These limitations are absolutely necessary in smaller communities if financial professionals are to continue their role in collaborative divorce. In order to promote consistency throughout the United States the proposed limitations must be implemented uniformly. If the permanent restrictions banning all future services by financial professionals are adopted, they will stifle and discourage financial processionals from the NFP role and will prevent the collaborative divorce process from realizing its full potential and changing the way society perceives divorce.

---

[41] "Model Rule of Professional Conduct" Rule 1.9 (2004), http://www. abanet.org/cpr/mrpc/rule_1_9.html.

CHAPTER 3

Complex Compensation Issues in a Divorce

Susan M. Mangiero and Lili A. Vasileff

INTRODUCTION

Divorce is seldom a happy event. Emotions run high, especially when there is a lot of money is at stake. After all, deciding on alimony and child support affects multiple lives for years to come. A cornerstone of this process is the identification and subsequent evaluation of assets and available income stream. Since many individuals are compensated with both wage and non-wage benefits, getting a final number can be time-consuming, arduous, and often requires the help of outside experts.

Three factors explain the challenge of assessing marital monies. First, organizations offer all sorts of benefits and terms can vary across employers. This is a consideration when trying to project future expected income and the value of non-wage benefits for an individual who is likely to change employers later on. Benefit amounts are often linked to the number of years with a company, job performance and/or financial health of the employer. Second, information about benefits may be hard to come by or difficult to interpret when it is available. Third, income may be unreported or overlooked and stay that way without the help of a forensic specialist.

The topic of compensation is broad. Entire books are written on the topic. What this article provides is an overview of compensation issues, a dis-

---

Susan M. Mangiero, PhD, AVA, CFA, FRM is a managing member of BVA, LLC, a business valuation and litigation support company.

Ms. Lili Vasileff, CFP™, CDFA is co-president of the Association for Divorce Financial Planners.

cussion of various types of compensation arrangements, information about data sources, and implications for financial planning and valuation, respectively.

OVERVIEW

Compensation arrangements are frequently classified by work status. Available benefits for a salaried employee can differ radically from those that accrue to a senior executive who has control over plan design, timing and amounts.[1] Closely-held firms enjoy a certain amount of flexibility in designing compensation plans for two reasons. First, they do not face the same accounting and tax rules. Secondly, public companies tend to be larger than many private firms. Benefits for big organizations have to reflect the often more diverse nature of the employee base in terms of job titles and a more structured human resources hierarchy of decision-makers.

If a spouse is a member of a union, benefits can be more or less generous than those offered to non-union employees of the same company. Compensation for self-employed persons can be radically different from wage earners and depends on the life cycle stage of both the company and the related industry. Someone might be a limited or general partner of a firm. Not everyone works in the business sector. For example, some individuals work for non-profit organizations. Others work for federal or state government agencies or perhaps are employed by the U.S. military. In each and every case, both wages and non-wage compensation will reflect the accepted practices for that type of employment situation.

Exhibits 1 and 2 illustrate the breakdown of compensation arrangements for a public company executive and private company business owner, respectively. While the executive of a public corporation will likely enjoy stock option awards and/or restricted stock grants, these benefits are not available to someone who works for a university or any other organization that does not fund operations by issuing common equity. For the business owner, wages may differ from market norms. The owner of a start-up could accept lower than normal wages in order to finance future expansion. On the other hand, wages and benefits for the owner of a mature company

---

[1] Executives generally have a greater need to manage tax liabilities. This means that benefit programs they help to create (or perhaps just influence) will not necessarily satisfy financial goals of non-executive employees.

may exceed typical payouts or take the form of excessive travel and entertainment expenses.[2] Either way, a business appraiser will look long and hard at company owner compensation when valuing full or partial ownership in a firm.

Exhibit 1
Sample Benefit Array for Public Company Officer

- Zero or low interest loans
- Executive stock options
- Restricted stock
- Deferred compensation
- Profit sharing
- Defined benefit pension plans
- Defined contribution pension plans
- Insurance: disability, health, life

Exhibit 2
Some Value Sources for Business Owner

- Officer compensation
- Pension plan benefits
- Perquisites
- Buy-sell agreement
- Non-compete agreements
- Key man life insurance policy
- Franchise value
- Distribution rights
- Personal goodwill
- Professional goodwill

---

[2] The term "value" means different things to different people. When an appraiser is hired to value any business interest, a standard of value is agreed upon at the outset. A common standard of value is "fair market value" which assumes a willing and informed hypothetical buyer and seller.

VALUATION ISSUES

Notwithstanding the notion that compensation arrangements can and often do vary by industry and organizational form, a cookie-cutter approach is ill-advised for purposes of valuing benefits for similarly titled individuals. Stock options owned by managers who work for private companies have a greater value if the probability of that company going public sometime soon is high.[3] Even then, marketability is an issue. Options issued by private companies are frequently much less liquid than options issued by public companies. This reduces their value. Furthermore, the marketability of options issued by public companies can vary too since some stocks trade infrequently. Subsidized loans are another case where valuation is directly determined by the detailed terms associated with the borrowing. Two executives at the same company can take out loans but the amounts, repayment requirements, rates, and restrictions on loan purpose can vary. The value of loan privileges is higher for someone who can borrow a large amount of money at an interest-free rate with a long time to repay the loan, if repayment is required at all.

Some companies allow higher ranking executives to craft their own compensation benefits, thereby empowering senior-level talent to pick things that coincide with their age or lifestyle, or allow them to take greater risks if they so desire. With self-directed choices, however, not every executive is on the same page and this can result in different paychecks for different executives. "Senior executives of Fortune 100 companies have the opportunity to participate in numerous plans. The financial planner, working with these executives, is challenged to identify and understand the key characteristics of each plan and how the employee can use these plans to achieve maximum financial security. ... It is common for senior executives to have 6 to 12 corporate plans simultaneously, each governed by different rules, growing at different rates and with different levels of contributions. The culmination of these plans can often account for one-third to two-thirds of an executive's annual compensation."[4] This choice factor likewise makes it impossible to generalize about executive benefits. By extension,

---

[3] There are many factors that determine the value of employee stock options. "Model Risk and Valuation" by Susan M. Mangiero (*Valuation Strategies*, March/April 2003 issue) provides an overview.

[4] "The Key to Working with Senior Executives: Understanding Corporate Plans" by Brett A. Coffman, CFP®, *Journal of Financial Planning*, October 2003.

valuing these benefits requires a clear understanding of the salient details that characterize executive benefits, not the least of which is the tax status of current and deferred income.

Business owners are a different story altogether, principally when they hold a majority stake and therefore have control over asset disposition, earnings stability, and dividend payments. As stated earlier, a founder might take a lower salary in the early years to ensure that adequate funds are available to fuel company growth. In other situations, owners can blur the line between personal and corporate benefits, compounding the problem of recognizing, and then analyzing, an individual's income and assets.

Divorce cases may require a departure from the fair market value standard to focus instead on the unique value of a company to the husband or wife.[5] This can occur when earnings from a business will be the primary source of funds for alimony and child support. State laws determine the standard of fair value, a standard that is often used in divorce cases in lieu of fair market value. Some laws seek to eliminate "double-dipping" so that the business value is considered only once. Other states ignore this concept. To illustrate, some states first require the valuation of a professional license or business, after which excess earnings over that value are computed for purposes of determining support capacity. Elsewhere, the business is valued as an available asset at the same time that the cash flow generated by the business is looked to for support purposes.

Generally speaking, anyone who fails to recognize the link between total compensation and work status – and the related impact on valuation – does a disservice to their client since amounts, timing, and likelihood of realizing income vary by employer and employer type. This is particularly true in recent years as the corporate benefit landscape continues to shift in response to economic pressures, new laws, altered demographics, and public outcry over excessive paychecks that do little to promote shareholder wealth creation. Even middle managers and blue-collar workers are affected as companies find it increasingly impossible to fund expensive promises and stay in business.[6]

---

[5] The standard of fair market value assumes a hypothetical, willing, and informed buyer and seller. This can differ from estimating value for a specific individual who has a particular reason for buying or selling an asset or entire business – i.e. keeping something in the family, tax reasons, gaining market share, etc.

[6] Byrnes, Nanette with David Welch, "The Benefits Trap", *Business Week*, July 19, 2004

Movement is afoot elsewhere as well. Municipalities are scaling back benefits to keep the tax burden in check. Union members regularly swap benefits for job security. This rapid change in the way people are paid directly influences estimates of future expected cash flow. This is particularly apropos for divorce cases that involve the long-range projection of earnings and cash flow, based in part on the current wage and non-wage benefit structure in place.

INFORMATION IS EVERYTHING

Two situations create problems. The first is having too little information about total compensation. The second is having too much information. Neither is ideal. When too little information is available, the financial professional must identify what is missing and seek it out. This can be challenging. For one thing, the information may simply not exist. Alternatively, it may exist but in a form that is difficult to rely on with confidence. For example, audited company statements can provide a lot more comfort to the user than those that are not audited. Yet even with audited statements, adjustments may be required to normalize financial data. This happens regularly with the appraisal of business interests. Owner compensation may be adjusted downward as part of the valuation analysis if competitors regularly pay lower amounts to managers. Automobiles or planes may be removed from the balance sheet if their use adds little to business earnings. Old inventory could be removed altogether if future use is unlikely in generating sales. These adjustments and many others permit a better assessment of the company's worth, a precursor to any divorce settlement that involves a spouse who owns all or part of a company.

The flip side is being deluged with information and not knowing the right way to sift through the details. Since many organizations offer an abundance of benefits from which the employee can choose, this outcome is not far removed from reality. Information is typically available for each benefit, either in brochure form or aggregated in a huge employee benefits handbook. A financial person may end up having to read about sponsor-provided pension plans, employee stock options, a variety of investment choices, insurance benefits and other perquisites such as education-related refunds, automobiles, health club memberships, interest-free loans, to name a few.

Even when such assets are easy to identify, the financial professional must know which questions to ask in order to properly assess income and adjust financial statements accordingly. When left undone, the result is an improper assessment of existing and estimated future earnings as well as a flawed picture of both historical and sustainable lifestyle. Deferred compensation is a case in point.

The tasks for understanding these benefits, available to highly compensated individuals, include financial discovery, reconciliation of reported income with actual cash flow, the unraveling of personal and business expenses, and the creation of a time line that lays out planned future accruals. Depending upon the employer's policies and IRS rules, these benefits may be transferable to an ex-spouse in the event of divorce; but many are not. Ferreting out information about "non-wage" benefits is hard work.

It is incumbent upon the financial professional brought in by the wife or husband to organize, gather and analyze all pertinent financial information. (Sometimes the mediator hires the financial planner and/or appraiser.) The objectives are threefold: 1) understand the client's historical lifestyle as a married couple, 2) interpret changes in their lifestyle during the divorce, and 3) project their needs on a post-divorce basis. Not surprisingly, this lifestyle analysis frequently provides more insight about available resources than an examination of official income reports. With wage earners, information is more readily available since the employer provides reportable income.

Information gathering is more problematic in the case of business ownership. As stated before, compensation may differ widely from accepted industry norms. An owner may expense items that relate to personal enjoyment and are not properly included as part of corporate financials. Moreover, an appraiser must be careful to distinguish business value from individual earnings.

Exhibit 3 lists some good places to find information, a precursor to the reconciliation of reported gross income with actual cash flow. Importantly, information gathering should take place at the time of the divorce, along with every year thereafter that defines the settlement period. In reality, the burden of disclosure is borne by the non-employee spouse, especially in the case of an acrimonious split.

Exhibit 3
Some Sources of Financial Information

- Personal & business income tax returns
- Limited partnership reports
- K-1 reports and underlying pages of detail
- Social security wages report
- Employee contracts
- Bonus letters
- Company insider stock transactions
- Direct deposit slips to employee's accounts (savings, broker)
- Deferred compensation benefit statements
- Retirement plan statements including summary plan description
- Payment of personal items by business (travel, entertainment)
- Subscription receipts
- Memberships dues slips
- Telephone account documents
- Company bank account statements
- Custodial accounts reports
- Trust documents
- Employee loan forms (indicated on pay stubs)
- Employee dividend reinvestment program reports
- Tax loss carryforward reports
- Margin loan information
- Company by-laws
- Buy-sell agreements
- Key man life insurance policy
- Foreign bank account statements
- Personal financial software files
- Company financial software files
- Travel itineraries

Sometimes, the non-employee spouse may be persuaded to offset his or her right to share in benefits by accepting other more tangible assets at the time of settlement. The reasons for offset are many but tend to focus on the goal of shielding the non-employee spouse from the uncertainty surrounding the valuation of future benefits. In this regard, many non-employee spouses consciously forgo upside potential gains from various benefit items based on conservative legal advice and their frequent need for immediate liquidity.

An additional consideration is the cost of having complex benefits appraised versus accepting real assets such as the marital residence, collectibles, or bank accounts. This posture may be appropriate in some cases but should not be based on less than full knowledge of the estimated value of such benefits. (Ironically, this estimate itself often requires the services of a professional appraiser.) Lastly, there is the emotional factor of staying tied to your ex-spouse in future years in order to enjoy one's legal claim when these benefits become available. Many non-employee ex-spouses are simply not up to the task of tracking the calendar or their ex-spouse's whereabouts to fulfill their entitlement to these benefits.

OTHER INCOME

A review of income tax returns is necessary but insufficient to fully understand what is at stake. Social security wage reports, pay stubs, and bank account statements help but are only a start. Ignoring all available and salient information can have dire consequences.

Consider Joe Smith. Income reports substantiate a consistently large salary. At the same time, the bank reports high credit card debt, repeated credit card advances, and a negative cash balance in the family checking account. The few marital assets that exist are hard to liquidate without incurring high fees. His wife, Sally, requests that generous support be awarded and points to income as the source, failing to take into account the marketability issue and the irregularity of available cash flows. Income information alone misses the mark. It says nothing about stock grants or option amounts, the tax status of existing benefits, cash flow requirements associated with transactions such as stock buys, and a bevy of other items.

Once other income is identified, the financial planner needs to look at regularity, predictability and amount. It is also necessary to understand the employer's contractual arrangements with the employee that dictate vesting rules, lock-out or black-out provisions, deferral issues, and anything else that limits the employee's ability to earn a living going forward.

ASSETS ARE IMPORTANT TOO

It takes significant time to become practiced in understanding a company's plans. Forging a relationship with a company's benefit manager is time well spent, especially if a large employer dominates the local economic scene. This person can provide invaluable information about whether and how often an employee can elect to change the benefit mix, tax issues, and related asset allocation issues. Beyond that, the financial professional must know whether and how an employee or business owner has hedged away financial risks.[7] Exhibit 4 is a checklist of action steps for anyone seeking a better understanding of an individual's asset base.

Exhibit 4
Asset Valuation Checklist

- Identify tangible assets.
- Identify intangible assets.
- Determine asset transferability rules.
- Assess liquidity of assets.
- Determine whether, how and if assets are likely to be forfeited.
- Evaluate whether assets can be hedged.
- If hedged, assess the risk-return characteristics of the hedge.
- Identify the tax consequences of transfering assets.
- Determine whether a spouse can cherry pick assets.
- Evaluate which assets can be offset against each other.

---

[7] Hedging transfers financial risk to a third party. Knowing exact details about the structure of the hedge is the only way to understand how the employee's risk position changes.

Complex Compensation Issues in a Divorce 41

An appraiser is often hired to provide an independent opinion of value for both tangible and intangible assets. Sometimes each spouse hires his or her own appraiser. Users may vary. It could be each respective attorney, a mediator, and/or the judge. Some assets are easier to value than others because a ready market already exists. Exhibit 5 lists some of the many items an appraiser could be called in to value.[8] Valuations are done for a host of reasons, not the least of which is determining worth for a divorce settlement.

**Exhibit 5
Some Items that Appraisers Value**

- Art
- Business goodwill, if applicable
- Coins
- Copyrights
- Majority ownership interest
- Minority ownership interest
- Non-compete agreements
- Patents
- Personal goodwill, if applicable
- Real estate
- Restricted stock
- Stock options

On a related note, hiring an appraiser can be a worthwhile exercise when putting together a pre-nuptial agreement, especially if an individual has been married before and already has children.

SUMMARY

Whether for financial planning or valuation purposes, understanding income and assets is critical to the divorce process. Many times, an attor-

---

[8] A business appraiser renders an independent opinion of value for business interests. Examples include, but are not limited to, employee stock options, restricted stock, patents, or minority (majority) ownership stake in a closely held company. Tangible asset specialists handle real estate, art, and machinery valuation.

ney will bring in both an appraiser and a financial planner because each person plays a unique role in determining what is available for distribution to the divorcing spouses. While a financial planner and appraiser each provide different services, they share some common responsibilities such as: 1) gathering information, 2) asking tough questions, 3) analyzing data, and 4) providing results to their client.[9]

The benefits landscape is already complex and unlikely to become any less so in the future. Add to that the vagaries specific to divorce and it is clear that specialists can provide some valuable help.

---

[9] Sometimes a divorce case requires the use of a forensic professional who can determine whether assets or income are missing or hidden on purpose. Importantly, the forensic work is done by someone other than the appraiser for many reasons, including the avoidance of conflict of interest.

CHAPTER 4

Valuing Professional Practices for Divorce Engagements: Reasonable Compensation and Excess Earnings – Hit or Myth?

Kevin R. Yeanoplos

There are no three words that create more fear and loathing in the hearts of business valuators than "excess earnings method" (EEM). Also called the "treasury method" or "formula approach," the "EEM" is the Rodney Dangerfield of valuation methods. Plain and simple, it gets no respect. Nonetheless, it is widely used to value professional practices in divorce engagements.

The IRS took a swipe at the EEM in Rev. Rul. 68-609:

> The "formula" approach may be used in determining the fair market value of intangible assets of a business only if there is no better basis available for making the determination.

The EEM has advantages as well as disadvantages, particularly when valuing professional practices for divorce engagements. The method is:

- widely used, and therefore recognized and at least partially understood by many people, including professionals and family law judges.

- logically quantifies the value of intangible assets by relating it to excess earnings of the practice.

Kevin R. Yeanoplos, CPA/ABV, ASA, is a principal with Yeanoplos Drysdale Group, PLLC, Tucson, Arizona.

- used to value practices for divorce engagements, separate the value of excess earnings, which becomes a marital asset available for distribution, from normal earnings (average earnings from similarly educated and experienced practitioners), which are used to estimate the appropriate amount of spousal support.

However, the method has several drawbacks as well. The EEM:

- is easily misapplied because it requires many subjective judgements on the part of the valuator.

- can understate the value of goodwill because it may not always factor in the going concern elements of a practice already in existence.

- In a marital dissolution, if excess earnings are used to reach a value estimate which is allocated between the parties, and is also included in the income stream used to set spousal support, it has been double counted. This is called the "double dip."

Even with its drawbacks, the method has much to offer. It provides a practical, formulaic approach to solving the valuation problem, while effectively combating the layperson's notion that valuation is all "smoke and mirrors."

Many valuators derive a great sense of security from this seemingly simple valuation blueprint. However, the subjectivity involved in applying the method often results in widely disparate conclusions.

The formula approach calls for the use of several key variables, such as a rate of return (discount or capitalization rate) and an earnings stream. Valuators often use objective empirical data to determine these variables. The same valuators may forget, however, that the subjective selection of objective data can mean the difference between excess earnings and no earnings.

Perhaps the single most important variable is the selection of a reasonable compensation. No single operating expense impacts the bottom-line profit as much as officers' compensation. Any approach that uses compensation in the derivation of enterprise earnings should be checked to ascertain that the compensation is reasonable. Otherwise, the approach could misrepresent profits as compensation.

The ultimate opinion of value can turn on the ability to support compensation for the practitioner. The expense that is deducted should represent the compensation that would be paid to the practitioner in an arm's-length arrangement for the duties and services performed. The following characteristics should be considered in addressing reasonable compensation:

1. Experience of the practitioner;
2. Hours worked on a daily or periodic basis;
3. Responsibilities of the position;
4. Duties performed regularly;
5. The age of the practitioner;
6. Nature of the practice;
7. Geographic setting of the practice;
8. Population of the practice area; and,
9. Revenues of the practice.

Rev. Rul. 68-609 provides some guidance in the selection process:

> The past earnings to which the formula is applied should fairly reflect the probable future earnings. Ordinarily, the period should not be less than five years, and abnormal years, whether above or below the average, should be eliminated. If the business is a sole proprietorship or partnership, there should be deducted from the earnings of the business a reasonable amount for services performed by the owner or partners engaged in the business.

The term *reasonable compensation* is derived from Section 162(a) of the Internal Revenue Code. Section 162(a) provides for a corporation to deduct as a business expense "a reasonable allowance for salaries or other compensation for personal services actually rendered."

As indicated earlier, one of the ways valuators generally judge the appropriateness of a practitioner's compensation is to look at what similar companies pay practitioners in similar positions. This can be extremely difficult, however, because no two practices are run exactly alike. In addition, private practices can be extremely reluctant to divulge what their top officers (often owners themselves) are actually earning as salary.

Regardless of the factors considered, it should be apparent that selecting a reasonable compensation requires a great deal of subjectivity. And to quote from Shakespeare, "there is the rub." One person's ceiling is another person's floor, one valuator's "reasonable" is another valuator's "outrageous." We would first do well to explore the reasons for using a "reasonable compensation" in the first place.

What has often been misunderstood by the lay community – the courts, lawyers, and parties to the divorce action – is that the difference between the value of a practice based on an earnings approach and the value of a practice based on a book value (or adjusted book value) is the value of the intangible assets, that is, goodwill and other intangible assets.

Understanding that the main goal in applying the formula approach is to quantify the subject company's intangible assets, the valuator should select a reasonable compensation that best allows for the isolation of the intangible value.

In selecting the reasonable compensation, there are many different options. For instance, in valuing a medical practice, a valuator can compare the subject professional to:

1. an employee physician in a large group practice;
2. an employee physician in a corporate practice;
3. the median physician in the United States;
4. the median physician in a particular region of the United States;
5. the median physician in United States metropolitan areas of certain populations;
6. the median physician of similar age or years in practice;

7. the median solo practitioner;

8. the median physician in the same specialty or subspecialty (including any permutations or combinations of the foregoing categories);

9. the "mean" physician in any of the foregoing categories; or,

10. some particular combination of the foregoing categories (if such data is available).

It is important to remember that "comparability" doesn't necessarily mean "perfect match." In many cases, it may be impractical or impossible to find a perfect match for a replacement compensation. At the same time, analyzing the underlying characteristics of the subject practitioner allows the valuator to select a replacement compensation that is both reasonable and defensible.

The valuator should select a replacement compensation that is comparable in terms of:

- type of professional service offered (some foster more repeat business than do others; some foster more referrals than do others);

- type of specialty, if any;

- practice location;

- age of the professional;

- nature and duration of the professional's practice, either as a sole proprietorship or as a member of a partnership or professional corporation;

- how fees are billed, i.e., insurance, government programs, patient/client pay, etc.;

- specific practitioner's hours worked and production;

- economic and demographic conditions in the practice's market area; and,

- number of locations the practice uses.

While it may require more research and resourcefulness in order to locate it, the most comparable replacement compensation for use in an excess earnings calculation may be that of an associate (i.e., a non-owner professional) working in the same city, with similar experience and training. Valuators can use personal and business contacts in order to determine such numbers.

CONCLUSION

The excess earnings method is perhaps underappreciated. It is widely used to value professional practices for divorce engagements. While many valuators may misapply the method, the correction application of the formula approach can provide an effective way to quantify the intangible assets of a professional practice.

An understanding of the reasons for selecting a reasonable replacement compensation is crucial to the correct application. If the valuator selects appropriate and reasonable replacement compensation, the chances for reaching a fairly stated valuation conclusion are enhanced tremendously.

CHAPTER 5

Unreported Income and Hidden Assets

Mark Kohn

Many divorce cases require some analysis to determine if there is unreported income and/or hidden assets. Quite often, the family owned business or professional practice is operated by one spouse, and that spouse has been under-reporting the true income. If his or her financial records are accepted as true, the amount of spousal support owed based on that artificially low income would be lower than it should be, and the value of that business will also be artificially lower because the value is usually directly related to the earned income of that business. Therefore, unreported income directly affects both spousal support and the property division. It therefore is important to investigate the probability of unreported income in divorce cases, but the process of finding and proving unreported income or hidden assets is often one of the most difficult assignments of a forensic professional, and the costs must be weighed carefully against the potential benefits. This article will present case histories that reflect the more common types of situations, some illustrative businesses, and suggest guidelines to use that are effective in determining unreported income and hidden assets.

THE CLOTHING MANUFACTURER

A gentleman from Korea owned a garment manufacturing business with reported income of approximately $75,000 per year. His wife held a position at a large professional firm and seemed both honest and competent with numbers. Wife proceeded to explain in detail that during the few years before separation, husband went to Korean hostess clubs several times a week, costing an average of $1,000 per night, husband spent large

---

Mark Kohn, CPA, CFE, CVA, ABV, is a forensic accountant specializing in marital dissolution litigation in the Los Angeles area.

sums gambling in Las Vegas, husband and wife acquired two residences, husband loaned $100,000 to his brother, husband and wife spent certain amounts for furniture for the residences and various other similar details. At the time of separation, wife found $50,000 in cash in several locations in the house, together with a note that detailed out the locations. A preliminary spreadsheet was made listing all of the various expenditures described by wife, and to that list were added items from the personal income tax returns, such as mortgage interest, property taxes, etc. Food and household supplies were not included because wife's income paid for these as well as other expenses. The preliminary conclusion was that husband was spending approximately $400,000 more than his after-tax salary. A review of the business records showed that the business was not loaning husband money, nor did it seem to be paying for the above described husband expenditures. A review of husband's bank statements did not show the expected $450,000 or so going through the account, and so the conclusion was that the husband was paying for the above expenses with cash. At that point it becomes the forensic accountant's responsibility to prove the unreported income in a manner convincing to a family law judge.

The approach taken was to first use the legal process and to then present several "pictures" or scenarios to the court. Subpoenas were issued to the institutions that provided the home loans and to the known bank accounts of husband. Husband's deposition was taken over a several day period, at which time he provided many boxes of records.

Husband testified that he usually gambled at a certain casino, whose records were then subpoenaed. Husband testified regarding certain transactions, much of which corroborated what wife had stated, even the cost of the dining room set. Husband testified that over the past few years, he had borrowed many hundreds of thousands of dollars from a few friends and relatives, and that he had no copies of the notes payable, and that he had made no payments on those loans.

An analysis of the company's financial records was made, comparing its ratios with similar businesses in that industry. It was noted that the gross profit of husband's business was significantly lower than that of the industry.

A lengthy report was then prepared for court. The introduction explained the issues, and then several scenarios were presented. The first was a schedule that presented the totality of what was known and alleged regarding husband's expenditures over the past three years. A second schedule compared the expenditures with the reported income. A third schedule detailed all of the amounts that husband claimed he had borrowed, with comments explaining how much was paid on those loans and other relevant details. A fourth schedule presented the company's income statement as is, together with the same income statement, side by side on the same sheet of paper, with one change – that the gross profit be changed to that of the industry, with the resulting increase in net income. It so happened that when the gross profit was adjusted to the norm, the additional income corresponded very well with the previously unexplained $400,000 of expenditures. Finally, documentation was provided that showed that many payments to husband's vendors were endorsed by a check cashing service. (This was noted when the backs of cancelled checks were reviewed while husband's deposition was taking place.) Therefore, a very plausible explanation of how husband received cash, and why his gross profit margins were so low, was explained by the fact that his costs of sales were artificially inflated. It seemed quite likely that checks were issued to his vendors and recorded as cost of goods sold, and then some of the vendors cashed the checks and returned the funds to husband, who then used the cash for his lifestyle.

Therefore, the report overall explained that on a reported low income, husband acquired two houses, he gambled heavily, he allegedly spent large sums on personal entertainment, and his explanations for where the money came from was extremely flimsy, while the explanation that it came from unreported business income was rather solid.

UNREPORTED BEER SALES

A large restaurant sold Southern food and beer, with the beer being sold in a prominent part of the restaurant. The beer sales were a major part of the business. The owner reported approximately $50,000 of annual income from the business, and yet he and his wife drove expensive cars, their children attended private schools, and husband was buying significant amounts of real estate.

Records of the local beer distributors were subpoenaed. Those records detailed exactly how much beer, and what types of beer (kegs, bottles, etc.) were sold to the restaurant during the prior two years. A forensic accountant went to the restaurant, ordered a drink at the bar, and took note of all of the prices of the beer by type (Bud, Miller, regular, light, etc) and size (8 oz, 12 oz, etc). The amount of beer purchased per the subpoenaed records of the beer distributor was then priced out. For example, if 1,000 cases of Miller ten-ounce light were purchased each year, and each case held 24 bottles, and that item would sell in his restaurant for $2.00, then the sales for that item would amount to $48,000 per year. After pricing out each item of the purchased beer, an expected total sales for the year figure was calculated. (Inventory was assumed to have remained constant at the beginning and the end of the year, and we adjusted the current prices to reflect probable lower prices for the prior year.) We then compared this calculated total sales of beer with what was reported on the books, and found that the reported sales was around five hundred thousand dollars lower than our calculated amount.

HOME IMPROVEMENTS

A manufacturer of personal products made massive improvements to his home, so that the additions were larger and more costly than the original structure. Extensive landscaping was also done, including the transplanting of large trees. An analysis of the personal banking records showed that the remodeling was not paid from personal funds. The business records were then analyzed, and it was noted that there were many corporate payments to home remodeling contractors and landscapers, but the supporting invoices all indicated that the work was done at the company. Even the massive landscaping invoices showed that the work was done at the company's office, which was located in an industrial park that had virtually no landscaping. Furthermore, the industrial park was not even owned by the company, so it was peculiar for the company to be apparently paying for the landscaping of someone else's property. Something was obviously out of order, but the necessary proof was missing.

The document production procedure being followed was that all of the documents requested were provided as photocopies. Because the home remodeling was apparently not paid by the homeowner or his business, which was bizarre, and because of the unusual landscaping situation, we specifically demanded the original home remodeling invoices. A forensic accountant was eventually shown the original invoices for all of the home remodeling, and it was clear that the job locations and some of the work descriptions had all been whited out and changed. When the whited out documents were held up to a light, the original writing was legible, and it showed that the remodeling work and the landscaping were done at the family residence. The remodeling deductions were added to the gross income available for support and to the valuation calculations.

THE HIDDEN FACTORY

During a valuation of a California manufacturing company, the document production was going very slowly, and then the forensic accountant was provided with approximately thirty boxes of documents at the opposing attorney's office. As expected, many of the boxes contained useless information. However, one box contained miscellaneous files, including correspondence between the company and its patent attorney. The file contained a letter from the company's patent attorney pointing out that the trademark of a particular unrelated Florida company was similar to a trademark of a product made "in the Atlanta facility." Until then, there had been no mention of an Atlanta facility, and nobody was aware of any business location besides the California facility.

THE WASTE MANAGEMENT COMPANY

A forensic accountant was asked to value a certain waste management business owned by a son of someone who also owned a waste management business. The son, hereafter referred to as husband, reported approximately $35,000 of income on his personal income tax returns for the three years before the date of valuation, and he had no corporate tax returns prepared for the business. When asked to produce general ledgers, paid bills, and accounts receivable records for the business, he was so uncooperative that a motion to compel was filed and upheld by the court. Records were still not produced, partially on the grounds that they did not exist, or records were produced with all of the important information blacked out. Counsel asked the forensic accountant to do the best he could under the circumstances.

Recognizing that the court was aware that husband was deliberating hiding information, and recognizing that no tax returns, financial statements, or accounts receivable were available, and recognizing that the waste management business is often quite lucrative, wife was asked to go through her diaries and photo albums and collect items that were requested. A lengthy report was then prepared consisting of approximately 25 color photos followed by a brief valuation report. The photos were all taken in the last few years before the date of valuation, and they included photos of the mink coats acquired, the huge new swimming pool built in the back yard, the new expensive furniture, wife's new Mercedes, wife's diamonds and pearls, children on the family yacht and family photos of Hawaiian vacations. The report explained that the above lifestyle was typical of someone who earned at least $500,000 a year of income, that amount was reduced somewhat simply to be conservative, and the resulting income was capitalized to arrive at the value of the business. It was obvious during trial that the above lifestyle was impossible on $35,000 a year, and husband's extreme non-cooperation made the above methodology not only necessary, but also believable.

The following three presentations are good examples of the methodology and techniques that could be used to find unreported income.

A LAW PRACTICE

Assume that a certain lawyer has what seems to be a successful practice, but reports low gross receipts and low net income. He also lives a lifestyle that indicates a much higher net income. Gifts, inheritances and loans are excluded as possible sources of income by discussions with the spouse and friends.

The investigation would start by obtaining the lawyer's accounts receivable records together with his cash receipts journals. A subpoena of the law practice's bank would produce the deposit offsets – the deposit slips that accompanied each deposit, together with the client checks that were deposited.

One would then compare all of the activity, as follows: First, one would compare the total collections for the year as reported on the accounts receivable records with the total collections reported on the tax return.

(The accounts receivable records would likely be correct, because the lawyer would not want to present false information to his clients.) If the total collected per the accounts receivable records should exceed the total reported, then the difference would be presumed to be unreported income.

One would then prepare a more detailed analysis. One would look at the billings for a certain month – for example, January. Assume that the lawyer billed Mr. Smith $5,000 for services rendered that month. One would then review the accounts receivable records for February for evidence of payment of the $5,000. One would then examine the subpoenaed bank records to see if the $5,000 was deposited.

The deposit offset could reflect a deposit of $5,000 less cash withdrawn at the teller's window for $3,000, as an example, for a net deposit of $2,000. It would thus be possible that only the $2,000 would be reported on the lawyer's cash receipts journal. If only $2,000 was reported on the cash receipts journal, sales for the year would be $3,000 less than actual. Perhaps the lawyer might repeat this type of activity many times during the year.

A follow-up step would be to review the lawyer's personal bank records and credit card charges. This might reflect virtually no amounts being spent for groceries, clothing, household supplies, etc. The absence of records of such expenditures, contrasted with a known lavish lifestyle, would mean that the lavish lifestyle is being paid for in cash. That cash might have come from those withdrawals at the teller window. The presentation of the accounts receivable analysis with the business bank records with the personal banking activity would be powerful evidence of unreported income.

THE COIN-OPERATED LAUNDROMAT

One of the most important costs in the coin-operated laundromat business is utilities – water and power. Assume that the business owner reports gross receipts of $1 million, and provides an income statement that reflects various expenses, including utilities expense of $350,000. That means that his financial statement reflects utilities expense to be 35% of sales.

The first step would be to obtain statistics from the industry to see if the subject business's numbers seem reasonable. If, in the industry, the typical ratio of utilities expense to sales is 20%, then one could presume that the subject business is under-reporting $750,000 of income. That would be computed by dividing $350,000 by 20% to arrive at expected sales of $1,750,000 – which is $750,000 higher than the amount reported.

The analyst should then validate the conclusion of $750,000 by investigating the personal lifestyle of the owner. An investigation of the actual laundromat machines might also be required. Data from manufacturers regarding how much water and electricity is used per load together with data from recently paid bills from the utility company would allow calculations of the typical water and electricity costs per load. Those costs should then be compared to the amount the laundromat charges to operate the machine per load.

The resulting ratio should be compared to the financial statements. For example, if the data supports a conclusion that it costs 60 cents in utility costs per load and the laundromat charges $3 per load, then the ratio is 20%. If the financial statements reflect a 30% ratio, one could presume that some income is unreported.

THE GARBAGE COLLECTION COMPANY

Assume that the business tax returns for a garbage collection company reflect low gross receipts and low net income. The family lifestyle, however, reflects significant income. Investigating this situation would require industry statistics, private investigators, and subpoenas.

One would first determine, from the tax returns or through a private investigator, the number of the company's collection trucks. From industry statistics, one would estimate the typical gross receipts earned per truck per year. One would then multiply the typical gross receipts per year by the number of trucks and compare that amount with the reported gross receipts.

The shortfall would presumably be unreported income. This could be bolstered by instructing the private investigator to follow various trucks through their daily routes to determine the names of the commercial customers being served. The customers could be subpoenaed to provide all payments made to the company within a certain period. The data on the subpoenaed records could be compared with the cash receipts journals of the subject company; any shortfall would be presumed to be unreported income.

It is important to note that in all of the above examples, the amount of unreported income was implied to be a relatively large amount. The above techniques are appropriate in such cases, because the conclusions are necessarily approximations. One could conclude that approximately $500,000 of unreported income exists, and that would be satisfactory in court, because the court would know that it might really be somewhere between $400,000 and $600,000.

If, however, one is looking for unreported income of $10,000 or a similar small amount, the effort would not be warranted by the costs, and the conclusion might be explained sufficiently by the other side to the court as to make the effort inconclusive.

TECHNIQUES USED TO FIND UNREPORTED INCOME AND HIDDEN ASSETS

The above examples demonstrate that finding unreported income and hidden assets is not a matter of guesswork. While success is never guaranteed, the use of certain techniques may produce successful results. Here are a few techniques to consider:

1. *Look at the lifestyle*
   One of the first steps is to look at the lifestyle of the person earning the income and match it with the income being reported. What kind of car does he/she drive and how was it paid for? What kind of clothes are being purchased, where does he travel and at which hotels does he stay? If there is a disparity between the lifestyle and the reported income, then one must look at the person's debt to see if the lifestyle is paid for by borrowed money. If the debt has not increased, one must look for other possible explanations, such as sales of hidden assets or a recent inheritance. If nothing seems to justify the lifestyle in excess of the reported income, then there is a good possibility that unreported

income is funding the lifestyle. This hypothesis, with its justifications, may not, by itself, be convincing to the court, but it will lend significant support to other evidence.

2. ***Look at the expenses***
Certain expenses are indicative of the nature of the business, and often they can be verified. In the above example of the restaurant, that business sold a huge amount of beer. Since there are only a small number of beer distributors and their records are typically computerized, it is relatively easy in such a situation to determine the volume of beer being purchased.

Many businesses have certain expenses that are directly connected to gross sales; those expenses should be given close attention. For example, certain manufacturing processes may require certain usage of utilities. A product that has water as a main ingredient, such as the manufacture of shampoo, will have production in direct relationship to the amount of water being used by the factory. A review of the company's utility bills may demonstrate whether production is going up or down. If the business records show that sales are down, production is down, but water usage is up, then that is evidence that sales are presumably not being reported.

3. ***Look at the cash flow***
How does the money come in and who receives it? If a certain person opens the mail, records what payments came in, and then delivers the checks to a second person, who actually makes the deposits, then there is reasonable internal control over the funds. In that situation, it is probable that all receipts are being recorded. In smaller businesses, such as in professional practices, it is possible for the same person to open the mail and to make the deposits, and it is not unusual for the owner himself to get the mail once in a while. Furthermore, payments are often made out to an individual instead of the formal business name. Particularly with a professional practice, the name of the person is often the name of the business, or a client may issue payment in the name of the partner who provided the services. In situations where the owner might open the mail and where checks could be payable to the owner, one should review the accounts receivable records with the cash receipts records. All write-offs of significant amounts

should be reviewed to see if the write-offs are merely cover-ups for receipts that were simply deposited into a personal bank account instead of the business account. The write-offs should be supported by documents indicating attempts to collect, such as correspondence, letters from the company's attorney, lawsuits, etc.

4. *Look at the business operations*
A visit to the business premises is very helpful, and sometimes it helps rule out certain areas which might otherwise he explored. For example, a business with gas stations has less of a probability of unreported income than a supermarket. A visit to the gas stations will show that all sales, in dollars, are reported by each gas pump. If the owner does not work at the gas station, he would not want the pump to malfunction, because that is his only way to determine that his employees are not stealing from him. Therefore, the pump equipment itself is very useful in determining the actual sales. In a supermarket, an owner could simply arrange that certain cash receipts be simply not deposited. It is essential to understand how the business is run, how often the owner comes to the business, what is his relationship with his employees, etc.

5. *Look at the industry ratios*
There are statistics available for many businesses, and the statistics of the subject business should be compared with others similar to it. In particular, the gross profit margins and the overall profitability should be compared. If in the industry, it costs fifty cents for each dollar of sales, and in the subject business, it costs sixty-five cents for every dollar of sales, then one should examine the expenses to see if they are inflated by personal or unusual expenses. It may be that there is a logical explanation for the variance of the subject business from the industry norm, but the variance itself is an indication that something is unusual, and deserving of special analysis.

6. *Consider using private investigators*
This can be quite expensive, but private investigators are useful in obtaining related physical observations or documentary support. In cases where there are suspicions of real estate being acquired secretly, or secret bank accounts, or, as mentioned above, the business trucks go to many customers, a private investigator could be

of great assistance. Private investigators also conduct trash searches, the results of which are sometimes of incredible benefit.

7. *The net worth method*
There is another method of uncovering unreported income that is theoretically very solid but sometimes difficult to use, and that is the method known as the net worth method. The net worth method has been used by the IRS, it still is being used by the IRS, and it was successfully used to convict Al Capone of income tax evasion (2 USTC 786). It works well in situations where there are known significant assets, such as real estate. In situations where there are not well known assets, such as unidentified Swiss bank accounts, this method will not work.

In brief, the method is very simple. An example will make it easier to understand. Imagine a person who had virtually no assets at the beginning of year 2000 and he had no debts either. During the years 2000, 2001 and 2002, he reported income of $50,000 per year. He lived modestly, with annual living expenses of approximately $50,000. Based on the above facts, one would expect that at the end of year 2002, he would be in exactly the same financial position that he was at the beginnging of year 2000 – no assets and no debts. Whatever he earned, he spent on living expenses. If it turns out that at the end of year 2002, he owned a house for which $400,000 was paid as the down payment, then one can make an initial presumption that the $400,000 was earned during the years 2000 and 2002 and was simply not reported anywhere. He had nothing in the beginning, and he somehow had $400,000 at the end, and so he must have earned it. One must make sure the analysis is as tight as possible, however, by trying to validate that he really had nothing at the beginning of the period, and that he did not receive the $400,000 as a gift or inheritance or loan.

The method consists of several steps. First, one identifies the known net worth of an individual at the beginning of a particular time period and the known net worth at the end of that period. The difference is the change in net worth. Net worth normally means the amount by which a person's total assets exceed their liabilities, but it has a slightly different meaning when used to uncover unreported income. For the purposes of uncovering unreported income, one must generally use the cost for each asset rather than the fair market value, so that one doesn't mix any natural growth into the calculations, such as stock market gains. Therefore, one determines the total assets at the beginning of the period based on what it cost to acquire those assets, and then one determines the assets at the end of the period based on what it cost to acquire those assets. One then adds the known living expenses – if money was spent, it had to come from somewhere, and since it was spent, it will not appear anywhere in the remaining net worth. The living expenses therefore represent funds spent that no longer exist. Finally, one subtracts the reported income, since that may account for funds used to increase the net worth or to pay for the living expenses.

Therefore, if a person's net worth increased over a five year period by $10 million on a cost basis – i.e., $10 million was spent on assets – and living expenses during that period were $2 million, and reported income was $3 million, then it's 10 plus 2 minus 3 = $9 million of unreported income. Looking at it backwards, one asks – how was it possible to spend $10 million on new asset purchases and another $2 million on living expenses, when the reported income was only $3 million?

The beauty of this method is that the logic is clear and the methodology is often easy to use. Sometimes the major part of the analysis is obtained simply from various subpoenaed financial statements prepared by the individual over a period of time.

The difficulties of this method include developing refutations to defenses raised by the accused, which will be explained shortly, and the difficulties one sometimes encounters when trying to determine what is really owned and what cash was used to acquire those assets. A person may have had very little assets at the beginning of a period, and an art collection at the end of the period. If he had no purchase invoices, and no payments by check from his known checking account, then one is left with an art collection that might be worth five million at the end of the period without any idea at all as to what was paid to acquire that collection. One may have to resort to conservative estimates in such a situation.

This method is most suited for situations where:

1. The subject maintains no books and records, or his books and records are unavailable, or the books and records are inadequate, or where the subject withholds his books and records, and,

2. The subject seems to have acquired a large amount of assets, or

3. The subject seems to have spent far more than he earned.

As is implied in the last comment made above, the net worth method is useful even if significant assets are not acquired, but excessive spending can be documented. The methodology is the same – one starts with beginning net worth, one calculates the amounts spent, and then one compares the sum of those amounts with what was reported as income. The difference is presumably unreported income. For example, if a person had no beginning net worth, and then he spent one million dollars over a two year period while reporting $50,000 a year of income during that period, he presumably had unreported income of $900,000. (This method is technically called the Expenditure Method, but it is a derivation of the Net Worth Method, and it is used by the government in its investigation of tax fraud and organized crime.)

There are several methods used by the accused to try to refute the conclusions reached by the net worth method.

The most frequent methods attempt to attack the conclusions head on. When the evidence indicates an unexplained increase in net worth, one asserts that there really was no increase at all, because one had that net worth all along. For example, when the evidence shows that a huge down payment was made on real estate at the same time as when the reported income seemed grossly insufficient, one asserts that the down payment came from cash that was hoarded at home under the mattress. This is not as ridiculous as it sounds, because unreported income must be proven, and so the proof should exclude that possibility to the extent possible. The IRS therefore trains its agents that if the net worth method is being used, the agent should first elicit from the suspect deposition testimony or other evidence that the assets at the beginning of the period did not contain secret assets such as cash under the mattress. One can also demonstrate that the subject earned very little income before the period of investigation began, and that his lifestyle was indicative of having accumulated very little cash.

The second most frequent method is to explain the increase in net worth by means of receipts of money in ways that do not constitute taxable income. The usual explanations are that one received a large inheritance, or that one's family gifted the money, or that one's family and/or friends loaned the money. If the person's family lives in the same state, where one can look at probate records or bank records, it is much easier to deal with than if the family lives in a foreign country. Subjects who have relatives in foreign countries will often claim that their large disbursements were funded by cash given to them whenever they visited their relatives abroad. They claim that they brought the money here in suitcases, or that their relatives gave their money to a third party, who arranged that American dollars would be handed to the subject upon his arrival back in the United States. They often argue that the assets that were acquired really belong to their foreign relatives, and they acquired the assets in their names only for convenience purposes.

While many of the claims that attempt to refute the net worth method appear nonsensical at first glance, it often requires significant analysis and legwork on the parts of the forensic accountant, private investigator, and attorney to find solid evidence that refutes those claims.

CONCLUSION

In summary, there are definite and very useful techniques that can be used to find hidden assets and unreported income. Quite often, enough evidence can be collected to present a very solid case. Sometimes, the evidence is not as solid but many clues are available that are very meaningful to a trained eye. The problem then becomes a matter of proving the allegation, rather than determining it.

CHAPTER 6

Equitable Distribution and Community Property States

Joyce C. Somerville

INTRODUCTION

Upon divorce the distribution of marital assets and debt will depend upon which state you resided in and the state in which you litigate. Either the community property laws or the principals of equitable distribution guide the distribution of assets.

HISTORY OF PROPERTY DISTRIBUTION

Property distribution upon divorce has gone through essentially three phases in the United States. The earliest phase was the "title distribution" phase of community property and common law. Most American states inherited their approach to property distribution from the English common law. Property was retained after divorce by the party who held title to the property. For many reasons, under common law most property belonged to husband.

The second phase was called the "discretionary distribution" phase. This was in response to the substantial disparity in economic consequences of divorced men and women. The divorce courts were now given tremendous discretion to divide any property held by either of the divorcing spouses.

The third and present phase is the "marital property equitable distribution" phase. Under marital property equitable distribution principles all

---

Joyce C. Somerville, CPA, is a manager of the Matrimonial Litigation Group of RosenfarbWinters, LLC in Tinton Falls, NJ.

property acquired during the marriage is considered marital property except if considered separate property. Separate property consists of the following:

- Inherited property – property inherited by one spouse is usually excluded from distribution in divorce whether received before or after the date of marriage.

- Property excluded by agreement – most states recognize prenuptial or postnuptial agreements, which exclude certain assets and liabilities from the marital estate.

- Property acquired prior to the marriage

- Compensation for personal injury – compensation received by one spouse as a result of personal injury is usually treated by most states as separate property

- Property acquired with the proceeds form the sale of separate property.

- Property acquired by gift.

- Property that qualifies as separate property for other reasons – for example some states consider disability benefits as separate property while other states treat nonvested property benefits as separate property of the spouse who earned them.

SEPARATE AND MARITAL PROPERTY

Separate property can be considered marital property if it becomes co-mingled with marital assets. Co-mingling occurs when separate property of one spouse is combined with marital property or separate property of the other spouse. Co-mingling may cause separate property to lose its identity and in turn its exempt status.

A forensic accountant is often engaged to assist in preparing a schedule of the "marital property." In addition, the forensic accountant may be asked to trace co-mingled property back to its origin as separate property and prove its exempt status.

An increase in value of exempt or separate property may be marital property. This is one of the most controversial topics relating to distribution of marital property. In general, most states treat the appreciation in one of following ways:

- Treated as separate property if the increase was not caused by any activity of either spouse.

- Treated as separate property regardless of whether the non-owner contributed toward the increase in value.

- Treated as marital property if it can be demonstrated that either spouse contributed toward the increase in value.

- Treated as marital property only if it can be demonstrated that the non-owner contributed toward the increase in value.

- Treated as marital property and is therefore subject to distribution regardless of how the increase in value came about.

A forensic accountant may be engaged to determine if any incremental appreciation was created during the marriage that must be considered in the divorce.

COMMUNITY PROPERTY STATES

Community property states generally split martial property equally between the husband and wife. However, the majority of states are equitable distribution states. In equitable distribution states the "marital property" is not necessary split equally but is divided equitably or fairly.

EQUITABLE DISTRIBUTION STATES

In equitable distribution states, a marriage is viewed as an economic partnership and the respective spouses make contributions to the success or failure of that partnership. The law does not provide a definition of what is equitable between spouses. There is no standard or formula. In these states, when a divorce is granted, the court determines how the "marital property" will be fairly distributed based on fifteen enumerated factors under the law as follows:

- The duration of the marriage,
- The age and physical and emotional health of the parties,
- The income or property brought to the marriage by each party,
- The standard of living established during the marriage,
- Any written agreement made by the parties before or during the marriage concerning an arrangement of property distribution,
- The income and earning capacity of each party including education background, training, employment skills, work experience, length of absence from the job market, custodial responsibilities for children, and the time and expense necessary to acquire sufficient education or training to enable the party to become self-supporting at a standard of living reasonably comparable to that enjoyed during the marriage,
- The contribution by each party to the education, training or earning power of the other,
- The contribution of each party to the acquisition, dissipation, preservation, depreciation or appreciation in the amount or value of the marital property, as well as the contribution of a party as a homemaker,
- The tax consequences of the proposed distribution to each party,
- The present value of the property,
- The need of a parent who has physical custody of a child to own or occupy the marital residence and to use or own the household effects,
- The debts and liabilities of the parties,
- The need for creation, now or in the future, of a trust fund to secure reasonably foreseeable medical or educational costs for a spouse or children, and
- Any other factors the court may deem relevant.

HOW DO COMMUNITY PROPERTY STATES DIFFER?

In community property states, the community or marital property are shared equally in the division of the marital estate in the event of a divorce. The law regarding property in community property states indicates that everything a husband and wife acquire once they are married (other than gift or inheritance) is considered community property and is equally owned by both parties, regardless of who provided the money to purchase the asset or whose name the asset is held in.

However, some community property states have started dividing marital property in a fair and equitable manner, rather than equally (with the spouse at fault in the ending of the marriage usually ends up with less than 50% of the community property). Community property states include: Arizona, California, Idaho, Louisiana, Nevada, New Mexico, Texas, Washington and Wisconsin.

One of the most important goals of the divorce process is to divide the marital property between two spouses. In general, most of the property owned by a divorcing couple is marital property (referred to as community property in nine states) that will be divided between the parities.

However, before the marital property can be properly allocated, the assets must be identified and valued. The issue of the distinction between separate and marital property can be very complex requiring an in depth review of financial records. The marital estate may also consist of a business a professional practice, stock options, retirement benefits, etc. and valuing these forms of marital property can be complicated and subjective. As a result, an experienced forensic accountant with specialized knowledge, training and experience in matrimonial accounting is often retained by the attorney and can be a crucial element in a divorce settlement team.

CHAPTER 7

Business Owner Investigative Techniques: A Focus on Fringe Benefits

James F. McNulty

The spouse of a professional (who owns a small or closely-held business) is at a distinct disadvantage when trying to investigate the tax or financial statements of the professional's business in a matrimonial divorce matter. Typically, the spouse will rely on the attorney to ask for the assistance of a competent and savvy forensic accountant specializing in investigative accounting. The forensic accountant is familiar with the concept that the true value of the business is only determined based upon a thorough examination and review of the underlying transactions within the business.

A significant amount of income is frequently hidden or disguised in the form of perquisites (i.e., fringe benefits that are labeled as business expenses but that in fact are personal expenses). The determination of whether a fringe benefit is deductible for tax purposes is not the controlling factor when analyzing the perquisite for matrimonial accounting.

The forensic accountant in a matrimonial engagement must search to uncover hidden income and identify perquisites. Without a complete search for the correct amount of fringe benefits (based upon state specific matrimonial guidelines) the amount of property distribution to the spouse will most certainly not be properly calculated.

The examination by a forensic accountant on the business of a spouse does not generally rise to the level of an Internal Revenue Service (IRS) examination. The overall conclusions reached between the two investiga-

---

James McNulty, CPA, CFSA, DABFA, Cr. FA, Partner, DiGabriele, McNulty & Co., LLC, Certified Public Accountants, Clark and West Orange, New Jersey.

tions are different since the standards and scope of the investigations are different. The purpose of an IRS examination is to determine if the returns filed were filed in compliance with the applicable laws within the Internal Revenue code. However, there are many correlations between the procedures and techniques in a forensic investigation of a matrimonial matter and those of an IRS examination of a tax return.

The most important similarity is the "procedures" or "techniques" for finding the results. The results may be dramatically different. For example, many of the items that would not be allowable for IRS purposes under the law would be acceptable for matrimonial purposes such as entertainment expense. Entertainment expense is limited under the IRS rules based upon the Internal Revenue code and related examination guidelines. In a matrimonial matter, entertainment expenses that are considered "personal" would be considered a perquisite that adds to the value of the business.

The forensic accountant should not shy away from the valuable procedures and techniques offered by the IRS in the examination of a business because of a fear of being considered overreaching and overzealous. The forensic accountant will better serve the client by using all available resources that provide the most accurate result. Obviously, while the level of investigation is generally not as comprehensive as an IRS audit, and the results in a matrimonial matter are given to the attorney, the forensic examination nevertheless requires an analysis that goes far beyond simply asking a few questions and completing a report.

One of the major parts of the analysis is the examination of the business of the spouse to locate and document the real income of the business. This is accomplished by locating any additional income in the form of perquisites that the business owner receives from the business. Coincidentally, these perquisites are most likely personal expenses that are not deductible for IRS purposes. Typically, the business owner is not properly reporting the perquisites as either an owners "draw" or as a "nondeductible" expense.

As previously illustrated, whether an item is deductible or not deductible for IRS purposes is not the determining factor of whether that item is a perquisite in a matrimonial matter. The discovery of perquisites in a matrimonial matter may have a critical impact on the calculation of the spouse's potential available alimony and child support to be paid by the business owner.

The forensic accountant must make a decision on whether a disbursement is a personal fringe benefit ("perquisite") or whether it is a legitimate business expense of the business. The forensic accountant who is valuing a professional's business should utilize all of the prior on-the-job experience of practicing as a forensic accountant in addition to the vast and valuable IRS audit examination techniques.

INVESTIGATIVE TECHNIQUES (PROCEDURES)

The purpose of this chapter is to provide extensive and detailed guidelines for techniques and procedures that can be used in conducting a matrimonial investigation of a business-owner so as to determine both the realistic income of the business-owner and the value of the related business(es).

An examination of the business of a spouse includes the accumulation of evidence and data for evaluating the accuracy of the professional business owner (spouse's) financial statement information provided. The evidence accumulated includes testimony from the business owner spouse, a thorough review of the books and records, and other possible documents from third parties. The forensic accountant also should not discount his or her "gut-feelings" or "observations" when conducting the investigation, and these should lead to seeking additional corroborative evidence.

It should be noted that it is important to obtain sufficient competent evidence to determine the accuracy of the professional business owners' data provided. The forensic accountant must determine the appropriate amount of evidence to accumulate and establish the proper depth of the examination. This decision is a matter of professional judgment and is important because of the prohibitive cost of examining and evaluating all available evidence. There are a number of factors to consider when establishing the depth of the examination (whether a matrimonial investigation or IRS exam) including:

> The risk that the the business owner has made errors that are individually or collectively material. The factors involved are addressed during the evaluation of the internal controls of the business operations.

The risk that the examination will fail to uncover material errors. The factors involved are the depth of the examination, the examination techniques used, the nature of the errors (intentional or unintentional), and the reliability of available evidence.

Methods for accumulating evidence include:

A. **Analytical Tests** – such as analysis of Balance Sheet items to identify large, unusual, or questionable accounts. Analytical tests use comparisons and relationships to isolate accounts and transactions that warrant further examination or to determine that further inquiry is not needed.

B. **Documentation** – such as examining the business owners' books and records to determine the content, accuracy, and to substantiate items claimed on the tax and financial statements. A broad definition of documentation, i.e., anything that may be relied upon as a basis of evidence, should be employed. Suitability of specific documentation should be discussed with the client attorney so that evidentiary standards upon which documents are substantiated is determined.

C. **Inquiry** – such as interviewing the business owner or third parties. Information from independent third parties can confirm or verify the accuracy of information presented by the business owner.

D. **Inspection** – such as physically examining the business owners' assets, e.g., inventory or securities.

E. **Observation** – such as conducting a tour of the business to observe the business owners' daily business operations.

F. **Testing** – such as tracing transactions to determine if they are correctly recorded and summarized in the business owners' books and records.

Factors to consider when choosing an examination technique are:

A. Will the examination technique provide the needed evidence?

B. Will the benefits derived from using a particular technique justify the associated costs to both the examiner and the spouse paying the cost of the exam?

C. Are there less expensive alternatives that will provide the same evidence?

ORAL INQUIRY (INTERVIEWING)

A. An interview is defined as a meeting between two persons and usually includes holding a formal consultation for the purpose of resolving or exploring issues.

B. Interviews are used to obtain leads, develop information, and establish evidence in a matrimonial matter.

C. Interviews provide information about the business owners' financial history, business operations, and books and records. Interviews are used to obtain information needed to reach informed judgments about the scope/depth of an examination and the resolution of issues. Interviews are used to develop information, and establish evidence in support of your conclusions.

D. In certain circumstances, interviews may be conducted so as to take testimony under oath.

Who to Interview?:

A. Interviews should always be held with the persons having the most knowledge concerning the total financial picture and history of the person or entity being examined. Therefore, the forensic accountant should always interview the business owner directly. There will be many instances when the business owner will request that you deal with the controller or outside accountant. This is typical and not out of the ordinary. The business owner is attempting to operate the business and the distraction of a matrimonial investigation is not a welcome matter. On the other hand, the forensic accountant cannot allow the business owner to be completely shielded from the important and appropriate questions that only the business owner can answer. So, while preliminary interviews with associates and agents of the business owner are helpful (see *Third Party Interviews* below), at the appropriate phase of the investigation an interview directly with the business owner is required.

Specialists required (when appropriate):

- A. Examiners should identify, in advance, all the persons the business owner will have present at an interview and ensure that the appropriate expertise is available.

- B. For example, if issues of a technical nature and outside the forensic accountant's area of expertise will be discussed at the interview, the specialists should be at the meeting.

Third Party Interviews:

- A. The forensic accountant, when allowable, should obtain testimony from third parties who can provide relevant information to determine the accuracy of information given by the business owner.

- B. The business owners' right to privacy will be protected when contacting third parties for information.

    1. Information should be collected, to the greatest extent practicable, directly from the business owner.

    2. No information will be collected or used with respect to the business owner that is not necessary and relevant or legally mandated.

Preparation and Planning for Interviewing:

- A. **Timing** – Proper timing of the interview is essential in obtaining information that is material in resolving a matrimonial matter.

- B. **Review Available Information** – Prior to any interview, the forensic accountant should review all the information and data he/she possesses relating to the matter. Such information may then be divided into three general categories:

    1. Information that can be documented, and is not in dispute need not be discussed,

    2. Information that may be documented, but is in dispute or is questionable, or points to additional areas of inquiry, and therefore needs to be discussed, and

    3. Information that must be developed by inquiry or testimony.

C. **Interview File** – An interview file, separate and distinct from the general engagement file, should be created. The interview file should contain only data or information arranged in the order it is to be discussed or covered in the interview. The less data the examiner has to cope with during the interview, the easier it will be for him/her to vary his/her line of questioning. It is very distracting and may even cause some confusion for the forensic accountant to delay the interview to find a document or an item in a voluminous file. However, the files should contain sufficient data to cover all the matters under discussion, provided it isn't unmanageable.

D. **Prepare Outline** – Before the interview, the forensic accountant should determine the goal of, or purpose for, questioning the business owner. The outline should contain only information that is relevant and material. Extraneous matter should be excluded because it may be confusing and may adversely affect the end desired. Important topics should be set off or underscored and related topics listed in their proper sequence. Specific questions should be kept to a minimum, since they tend to reduce the flexibility of the forensic accountant.

Types of Interviews:

A. **Initial Interviews** – The initial interview should be held as soon as possible after retained being by the attorney or spouse.

B. **Subsequent Interviews** – Subsequent interviews with the business owners' spouse should be held if:

1. The business owner does not provide all the information requested;

2. More detailed explanations are needed; or

3. A review of the progress of the investigation is needed. The review should address information provided to date as well as out-standing information needed to complete the investigation.

C. **Third Party Interviews** – Additional third party interviews may be necessary when the business owner does not or cannot provide documentation regarding a transaction, a deduction, or an income item.

Documenting Interviews:

A. Interviews provide information not available from other sources. A properly planned and executed interview will provide an understanding of the business owners' financial history, business operations, and accounting records.

B. The engagement file should reflect in-depth planned interviews throughout the investigation. Sufficient questions should be asked to gain a clear understanding of the business owner, as well as the operations of the business owner.

C. The elements of an adequately documented interview include:

   1. Interview plan to address specific items required related to the business owner being interviewed. The type of return, financial statements, and relevant facts and circumstances are considered in the interview plan.

   2. The forensic accountant must go into sufficient depth to obtain a clear understanding of the nature of the business owners' financial history, business history, and day-to-day operations.

D. Questions of financial status or overall assessment of tax return validity, when appropriate.

E. Description of books and records maintained and their availability.

F. Complete explanation of the business owners' accounting system and accounting methods, including any changes when appropriate. This may also include an explanation of the accounting method used for taxes, if different from book accounting, and any adjustments that were made.

G. Explanation of the internal controls of the business.

H. The forensic accountant should take brief notes during the interview for significant responses to questions, and note those areas which may require additional development.

I. It is not advisable to take extensive notes during the interview. It can be distracting and hinder the flow of the interview.

J. As an alternative, questionnaires may be used to record taxpayer responses instead of a memorandum. If an interview questionnaire is used, the forensic accountant should ask follow-up questions as needed. The original questions and responses should be included in the file.

Interview Techniques:

A. Interviews provide information about the business owners' financial history, business operations, and books and records that are not available from other sources. Interviews should be used to obtain information needed to make informed judgments about the scope and depth of the investigation and correctly resolve issues.

B. It is important to create an environment where the business owner feels comfortable. The forensic accountant should maintain a friendly and professional demeanor. Suggestions for establishing rapport include:

   1. The forensic accountant should introduce themselves.

   2. The forensic accountant should explain what will happen during the investigation, and the purpose of the specific interview.

   3. The forensic accountant should recognize that a matrimonial matter is a sensitive matter and therefore the business owner may be tense or nervous.

   4. The forensic accountant should exhibit openness, honesty, and integrity, and be calm and objective.

   5. The forensic accountant should listen carefully to all details, be receptive to all information volunteered, regardless of its nature, and be patient and persistent in extracting the facts necessary to achieve the goals of the interview.

Conducting the Interview:

A. **Be Adaptable and Flexible** – The forensic accountant should keep an open mind. He or she should be receptive to all information provided, regardless of the nature, and should be prepared to develop it. If he or she is not flexible, he or she may waste a great deal of time and ask unnecessary questions, resulting in a voluminous statement of little or no value. Although the forensic accountant may find it easier to adhere to a fixed pattern of interviewing, or to rely upon a series of questions or topics, rigid adherence to any notes or outline will seriously handicap his or her flexibility. The outline and data should serve only as aids and not as substitutes for original and spontaneous questioning. A carefully planned outline will provide enough leeway to allow the investigator to better cope with any situation that may occur.

B. **Follow Through** – Incomplete and unresponsive answers have little or no value. Any answer, apparently relative to a pertinent matter, that is not complete and to the point should be followed up by questioning the business owner about all knowledge he or she has concerning every facet of the topic. The forensic accountant should follow through on every pertinent lead and incomplete answer. He or she should continue asking questions until all information which can reasonably be expected has been secured.

C. The following suggestions will help the forensic accountant to follow-through and obtain answers that are complete and accurate:

1. Use short questions confined to one topic that can be clearly and easily understood.

2. Ask questions that require narrative answers, avoiding questions that prompt only "yes" and "no" answers, whenever possible (see *Question Construction* below).

3. Whenever possible, avoid questions that suggest part of the answer (i.e., leading questions).

4. Be alert so as to prevent the business owner from aimlessly wandering. Where possible, require a direct response.

5. Prevent the business owner from leading the investigator off the point in question. He or she should not be allowed to confuse the issue and leave basic questions unanswered.

6. Concentrate more on the answers of the business owner than on the next question.

7. To avoid an unrelated and incomplete chronology, the forensic accountant should clearly understand each answer and ensure that any lack of clarity is eliminated before continuing.

8. When all important points have been resolved, terminate the interview. If possible, leave the door open for further meetings with the subject.

D. Maintain control of the interview; the forensic accountant should establish the pace and direction. Continually assess whether the business owner is providing pertinent information or is simply rambling.

Question Construction:

A. The areas to be addressed during the interview should be based on analyses completed prior to conducting the interview. Questions are the principal tools of interviewing.

B. There are four types of questions: open-ended, closed-ended, probing, and leading. Each is described below:

1. An open-ended question is one that generally requires more than a simple "yes," "no," or one or two word response in order to provide an intelligible answer. Open-ended questions often begin with What or How. For example:

   - "What are some of the characteristics that you look for in an employee?"
   - "How are walk-in customer transactions recorded?"
   - "Could you tell me about the month-end closing process that the business uses?"

   Open-ended questions encourage continued conversation and are often perceived as less threatening and therefore generally encourage a less restrained response.

2. A closed-end question is one that limits the response to a yes, no, or other simple statement of fact. For example:

   - "Do you have company paid life insurance?"
   - "Who is responsible for the month-end closing of books?"

- "Is that the company vehicle parked out front?"

Closed-end questions are useful to confirm understandings, establish facts, and to direct the conversation.

3. A probing question is generally a narrower or more focused version of an open-ended question. For example:

    - "Are cash and credit transactions of walk-in customers handled any differently?"
    - "How are monthly cut-off dates decided?"
    - "What happens next?"

    Probing questions are generally used for follow-up or to narrow the focus of a response to a particular area.

4. A leading question is one that includes a presupposition of some sort on the part of the questioner. For example.

    - "It would be better to park the company car in a more secure location, don't you think?"
    - "It's hard to find employees you can trust, isn't it?"
    - "Your husband doesn't appreciate what it costs to put in these long hours, does he?"

    Leading questions are those that seemingly convey an impression or opinion of the questioner, and are therefore dangerous to use because the respondent may simply provide a response which he or she feels is what the questioner wants. Moreover, some practitioners believe that the use of leading questions is unethical, especially those that suggest an opinion that is in fact not the true disposition of the questioner, but only a facade intended to trick the respondent. For these and other reasons, responses to leading questions are generally deemed unreliable in and of themselves.

C. Use the interview plan as a guide, not as an inflexible outline. Allow flexibility to respond to new information as it is received and to ask follow-up questions when clarification is needed.

D. Vary the types of questions and pause between questions. This technique can help establish a more conversational atmosphere.

Obtain as much information as possible during an interview. There may not be an opportunity to conduct another interview.

Listening Skills:

    A. The question, no matter how important, becomes irrelevant if the response is not accurately understood. Ways to enhance listening include:

        1. Making sure that non-verbal communication contributes to a comfortable atmosphere. If the investigator appears overly relaxed and is not looking at the business owner, the business owner may believe the investigator is not interested and will respond accordingly.

        2. Listening for the meaning of words. If the business owners' response is unclear, try paraphrasing or repeating what was said. Seek confirmation and expansion upon any summarization.

        3. Not interrupting the business owner and allowing a brief pause at the end of the response. Use the time to analyze the response and, if appropriate, formulate a follow-up question.

        4. Maintaining eye contact with the business owner. This demonstrates interest and non-verbal responses can be observed.

INSPECTIONS OF BUSINESSES AND RESIDENCES

    A. The physical observation of the business owners' operation, or tour of business site, is an integral part of the investigation process. Viewing the business owners' facilities and observing business activities is an opportunity to:

        1. Acquire an overview of the business operation,

        2. Establish that the books and records accurately reflect actual business operations,

        3. Observe and test internal controls,

        4. Clarify information obtained through interviews, and

        5. Identify potential unreported income issues.

Conducting Tours of Business Sites:

A. Tours of business sites should be conducted during examinations of all business entities of the business owner. Generally, the principal location, and any locations acquired during the period under investigation, should be visited. However, consideration should be given to the cost effectiveness and practicality of conducting the tour. When appropriate, alternatives should be considered.

B. Tours should be conducted after the initial interview and early in the investigation process. This clarifies what was said during the interview and provides a frame of reference when interpreting information in the books and records.

C. Tours should be conducted with knowledgeable individuals. The business owner, or their representatives, can often explain business practices that may initially appear unusual to the forensic accountant.

D. Tours should be planned to address large, unusual, or questionable items identified during the interviews.

E. Tours should not disrupt business operations or interfere with the business owners' interactions with customers.

Audit Techniques for Tours of Business Sites:

A. Observe and be alert to the physical surroundings. Confirm that assets identified on the tax return or financial statements are physically present and identify assets that are physically present but are not represented on the tax return or financial statements.

B. Ask questions to confirm understanding of what is observed and avoid confusion.

C. Trace common business transactions through the system. Look for discrepancies between what the transactions "should" look like and what actually happens. Look for weaknesses in the internal controls such as a lack of separation of duties. An evaluation of internal controls is critical in that it helps to determine the degree of reliance that can be placed on the books and records, and what additional investigative steps will be needed.

Inspection of a Taxpayer's Residence:

A. A forensic accountant may consider inspecting the business owners' residence. Due to privacy issues and the intrusiveness of such inspections, their use should be limited. The purpose of inspecting the business owners' residence includes (but is not limited to):

   1. Determining the validity of deductions for an office or business located in the residence.

   2. Determining the business owners' financial status.

Other Inspections of the Taxpayer's Residence:

A. When determining the business owners' financial status, an inspection of the interior of the home is not required. The following techniques are suitable alternatives:

   1. Ownership, sales price and mortgage information can be obtained from public records.

   2. The forensic accountant can drive through the business owners' neighborhood to gain a general approximation of the business owners' standard of living.

B. These activities should be completed early in the investigation process. Coordination with the business owner is not necessary.

EVALUATING THE TAXPAYER'S INTERNAL CONTROLS:

A. Many of the businesses of business owners' will likely be sole proprietorships or small, closely-held corporations. In these environments, the owner-managers usually control the entire operation through direct supervision of the business activities. It is not uncommon for one person or a small group of people to have the ability to override vital elements of a system of internal controls. Even in this environment, however, it is essential to evaluate internal controls to determine the appropriate audit techniques to be used during the investigation.

B. The evaluation of internal controls will assist the forensic accountant in determining the accuracy and reliability of the business owners' books and records. Additionally, the evaluation of internal controls should be part of the decision making process used to select the appropriate method for the examination of income and expenses. The forensic accountant should consider the type of business, the type of records maintained, and the business owners' financial status, and not just the income and expenses reflected on the tax return or financial statement.

Purpose of Evaluating Internal Controls:

A. An evaluation of a business owners' internal controls is necessary to determine the reliability of the books and records.

B. It is essential to evaluate internal controls to determine the appropriate investigative techniques to be used during the investigation.

C. An evaluation of internal controls is used to determine the scope of an investigation and the extent of audit procedures to be used.

D. An evaluation of internal controls is used to assess the level of control risk and establish the depth of the investigation. "Control risk" is defined as the risk that a material misstatement could occur and it will not be prevented or detected on a timely basis by the business's internal control structure, policies or procedures. The greater the control risk, the less reliability may be placed upon statements and reports generated by the financial reporting system of the business entity.

Evaluation of Internal Controls in a Small Business Environment:

A. Internal controls are often limited to the consideration of controls for segregation of duties and safeguarding assets. With this limited perspective, the evaluation of internal controls in small businesses are evaluations of internal controls in small businesses are often viewed as unimportant because control procedures in such environments are often weak or non-existent. This may be due to cost factors, lack of staffing, or a lack of concern with this aspect of the business.

B. The fact that internal controls may be weak in a small business environment does not preclude the necessity of determining the reliability of the books and records. Every business owner has a method of conducting business and safeguarding business operations.

Key Steps for Evaluating Internal Controls:

A. Internal Controls are defined as the "business owners' policies and procedures to identify, measure and safeguard business operations and avoid material misstatements of financial information."

B. The evaluation of internal controls can be described as an analysis completed by the forensic accountant which supports a broad understanding of the entire business operation.

C. The forensic accountant should obtain an understanding of three key elements of the business owners' business:

   1. The control environment,

   2. The accounting system, and

   3. The control procedures.

Control Environment:

A. To make an assessment of the control environment, the forensic accountant must understand, in detail, how the business operates. Therefore, the first step is to obtain overview of business operations. Interviewing the business owner and/or representative and touring the business are integral steps.

B. With the broad understanding of the business operation in mind, the forensic accountant must then seek to understand the control environment of the business. The control environment is made up of many factors that affect the policies and procedures of the business, including:

   1. Management philosophy,

   2. Management operating style,

   3. Organizational structure,

   4. Personnel policies, and

   5. External influences that affect the business.

Accounting System:

A. The second key area of internal control that the forensic accountant must understand is the business owners' accounting system. Gaining knowledge of the accounting system provides information about many of the business owners' transactions.

B. The forensic accountant should become familiar with the normal flow of each type of transaction, including:

 1. The accounting records which are involved in the processing, and

 2. Reporting of transactions.

 3. The recordation of the transaction from its initiation to its inclusion in the tax return or financial statement, and

 4. The flow of funds into or out of the business.

B. The forensic accountant must acquire knowledge of how the business operates on a day-to-day basis with respect to customers, suppliers, management, sales, work performed, pricing, location, employees, assets used, production and recordkeeping.

Control Procedures:

A. Control procedures are the policies and procedures established by management to achieve the objectives of the business. The control procedures are the methods established to assure that the business operates as intended. Separation of duties is the primary control procedure that concerns the forensic accountant. If properly executed, separation of duties will reduce the opportunity for any person to both perpetrate and conceal errors or irregularities in the normal course of their duties. Other specific procedures include:

 1. Documentation of procedures and transactions,

 2. Supervision of work and periodic review by independent third parties, and

 3. Timely recording of all transactions.

B. Many small businesses have one owner and no employees. Although no separation of duties can exist in this situation, other control procedures might be in place to assure accurate reporting of income and expenses. The greater the number of employees, and the more complex the structure of the business, the more likely some formal control procedures will exist.

Cash Businesses:

A. Many small businesses that deal almost exclusively in cash are likely to have few internal controls. Practically all income is received in cash. No independent third parties review the operation. Many expenses are paid in cash and documentation for transactions is often lacking.

Summary of Internal Control Evaluations:

An investigation of the business owner cannot be undertaken without an overview of the entire operation. An in-depth review of business owners' financial status can only be accomplished through an evaluation and documentation of internal controls, including the control environment, the accounting system and the control procedures.

Evaluation Methods and Tests:

A. **Document the Business Operation** – Draw-up an overview of the business operations. At a minimum, the information obtained should depict by whom, with what, how many, where, when and how business is transacted.

B. **Document the Accounting System** – Identify what books and records are maintained. At a minimum the forensic accountant should determine:

1. What the books of original entry are, whether they are automated, what types of subsidiary records (invoices, etc.) are maintained, what kinds of reports are prepared, how often they are prepared, and by whom.

2. How income is received, how expenses are paid, and who is responsible for receiving and recording income and expenses.

3. Who opens mail, deposits funds, writes checks, approves expenditures (both regular and extraordinary), signs checks,

makes book entries, prepares invoices, matches invoices, has access to cash registers, and receives and reconciles bank statements.

C. **Document Assets** – Identify the business owners' business and personal assets, including capital acquisitions, bank accounts and cash. At a minimum, the business owner and/or representative should be questioned regarding capital asset transactions, cash in bank, cash on hand, bartering, number and location of bank accounts, non-taxable sources of funds, and total assets held.

D. **Document the Flow of Transactions** – Outline the flow of receipts and expenditures through the books and records. Are there changes in the books? Is there a system of accounting for non-taxable receipts? Do the books and records have a system of accounting for cash receipts and expenditures? Does the business owner rely on information generated by third parties? Does the business owner use the books and records for purposes other than tax? Do the books and records reflect regulatory or licensing requirements?

Interview Techniques:

A. Most of the knowledge needed to evaluate the control structure of the business is acquired through interviews of individuals having first-hand knowledge of the business or through observations of the business operations. An in-depth interview of the owner of the business who is usually involved with every facet of the business is an excellent way to gain insight into the control structure.

B. While interviewing the business owner is ideal, the forensic accountant cannot require a business owner to accompany an authorized representative to an investigative interview. The forensic accountant should, however, request the business owners' voluntary presence through the representative.

C. When dealing with an individual who may be attempting to distort or conceal information, any information obtained through the interview process should be verified through tests of controls, such as the inspection of documents and reports or observations of the business operation.

Reliable Books and Records:

A. If it is determined that the business owners' books are reliable, the investigation of income can include direct testing of the business owners' books and records. Some examples of procedures using books and records are:

    1. Tracing specific items to receipts,

    2. Testing sample receipts to books and records,

    3. Applying the business owners' mark-up to expenditures per records,

    4. Testing sample client accounts to receipts,

    5. Analyzing adjusting journal entries and differences between books and the tax return or financial statement.

IDENTIFYING FRINGE BENEFITS ("PERQUISITES")

Now that the forensic accountant is well equipped with the tools to properly investigate the business in question, a list of the most common fringe benefits among business owners' would be helpful:

Automobiles and Auto Expenses

The most commonly reported method of providing for a company car and expenses is full company ownership or lease, plus full company-supported vehicle operation and maintenance, with the vehicle replaced every three or four years.

Gasoline credit cards are also often provided to family members of the business owner. When auditing for the gasoline credit card fringe benefit, be aware of the signatures on the credit cards as well as the vehicle license plate number and the location of the service station. Also determine whether all members of the family are having their automobiles repaired and serviced, with the bills paid by the company. Finally, check for additional autos leased to family members.

Health, Disability, and Other Insurance

A review must be made of all medical, health, dental, and life insurance costs to determine how much "free" insurance the business owner is receiving as a fringe benefit, since this represents a special benefit and additional compensation.

It is also important to note whether the company is paying for the business owners' personal automobile, homeowners, and umbrella insurances.

Club Dues and Expenses

When used to develop, conduct, and maintain necessary business relationships, 50 percent of club expenditures are generally considered a reasonable expense.

Non-business Entertainment

Very often a search of petty cash and credit card charges will reveal that the business owner is going out to lunch with friends, family, and non-business-related associates. Often these are not necessary and ordinary business expenses. Sometimes you will see a description of the alleged business activity and the names of the persons "entertained." However, further investigation may reveal that such "entertainment" occurred during a holiday or on a Saturday or Sunday evening, which are dates when such business activities do not generally occur, and may indicate the need for further scrutiny.

Pension, Profit-Sharing, and Deferred Compensation Plans

Supplemental retirement benefits amount to special deferred compensation arrangements not subject to taxation as current income. These deferred payments have the effect of augmenting normal retirement benefits as provided by Social Security and qualified profit-sharing and defined-benefit retirement plans. They should be considered as a fringe benefit and added to regular salary compensation.

Interest-Free or Low-Interest-Rate Loans

The invisible fringe benefit of granting free or low-interest-rate loans is not new, but it becomes more prevalent in years when there is a rise in interest rates. An analysis of the loans payable account often reveals such low-interest-rate loans. Even with tax changes as to favorable interest rate loans, the business owner still enjoys the benefits of this tax-free fringe benefit.

Unreported and/or Concealed Income

Consideration of unreported and/or concealed income is especially important in health care practices and other small business entities where cash is received. An examination of patient or client files is often very revealing. Inspect the deposit ticket, and note whether cash is deposited. Often a clue to unreported income is whether the deposit tickets reveal only checks (and never cash) being deposited. Verify that deposits are reconcilable to reported fee income through the bank statements. Also check the reliability of gross profit percentage rates and inventory turnover ratios against industry standards. Also seek to determine if checks made payable to "petty cash" are prepared on a regular weekly or monthly basis, endorsed by the owner, and charged to the expense of the business. Since uniform petty expenses do not typically occur on regular basis, such regularly occurring "reimbursements" are often indicative of unreported income. Finally, interview the nonprofessional spouse and/or terminated disgruntled employees for clues as to "skimming."

Nonworking Family Members on Payroll

Check Internal Revenue Form 941 or the W-2s for relatives or family members, especially parents, spouses, girlfriends, or younger children who are on the payroll at lower tax rates but who are not really working.

Personal Telephone, Electric, and Utility Bills

Obtain the various telephone numbers and addresses on utility bills in order to determine which are businesses and which are personal expenses, and cross-check these to paid invoices. Very often vacation home expenditures are written off against business income.

FEES AND OTHER MISCELLANEOUS CHARGES

The retainer and other personal legal fees for a divorce are frequently deducted in the cash disbursement journals as a business expense.

Check to see whether expenses like the mortgage for the home or the cost of the landscaper, the chauffeur, home repairs, and pool maintenance are being written off on the books of the business.

Bartered Goods or Services

Be aware of the professional who "barters" his professional services, for example, a dentist bartering dental cleanings for lunches at his patient's restaurant. Is the accountant bartering his fees to his electrician client for electrical services in the accountant's personal residence? If the dentist and the accountant are bartering their services, they are saving tax dollars, albeit illegally, and this represents additional business income.

MISCELLANEOUS

When searching for the "true" income of a professional or small business owner, also keep in mind the following:

- payments for weddings or special parties for relatives
- personal purchases of food, liquor, and so forth by the owner with business funds
- college tuition for children of employees
- personal use of boats or airplanes
- non-business gifts and flowers
- vacation travel expense
- purchase of personal furniture, jewelry, clothing, and the like
- maid and cleaning services at the personal residence
- payments for tickets to the theater, sporting events, and so on that are for personal use
- tennis or golf lessons
- checks made payable to the business owner or to "cash" and charged to expenses

CONCLUSION

Many of the above types of expenditures are legitimate business expenses. In fact, many an important business deal is made over a two-martini lunch, and business dealings are discussed at country clubs and on boats. Professionals do conduct work on weekends and evenings. However, we also know that many professionals and executives, particularly those in a cash business or in a professional practice, have a tendency to take advantage of charging off "tax-free" expenses that are non-business-related. The latter must be uncovered to determine "true" income available for alimony and support payments, and to determine the ultimate profitability of the practice. Increasing a spouse's income by the perquisites discovered in a forensic examination aids in arriving at "real" income, and also assists in the computation of true earnings when determining the value of the practice.

CHAPTER 8

Factors to Consider Regarding Division of Non-Marital and Marital Assets for Divorce

Richard A. Campanella and **Joseph M. Lo Campo**

INTRODUCTION

A couple has filed for divorce. They are going through the most difficult time of their lives emotionally and financially. They have accumulated during their marriage various types of assets and debts. The goal is to figure out, in a fair manner, their respective share of the assets and debts.

The ultimate determination of what is or is not either marital or non-marital property is the prerogative of the various legislatures and courts of the respective States. Forensic accounting practitioners are reminded to never attempt or assume these determinations themselves - such is the domain of the attorney. Nevertheless, an understanding of some of the more general principles relating to marital and non-marital property is helpful for practitioners so that they may plan and deliver more efficient and effective services on behalf of the client. Early and open communication with the appropriate state licensed attorney, prior to developing formulaic assumptions or performing requisite calculations, is required.

All assets owned by a husband and spouse, jointly or individually, are either marital or non-marital in character. In some cases, property may even be part marital and part non-marital in character. Non-marital property is, with a few exceptions, all premarital property (all you own free and clear

---

Richard A. Campanella, CPA, Partner, Director of Accounting & Due Diligence Services for DiGabriele, McNulty & Co., LLC, West Orange, New Jersey.
Joseph M. Lo Campo, Seton Hall University, South Orange, New Jersey.

up to the date of your marriage), all property that was received as a gift, or that was inherited. Marital property is everything else that you or your spouse (or both of you together) acquire after you say "I do." If you win the lottery and are awarded the money a few hours before the wedding ceremony, the prize money is your non-marital property. If you are awarded the money anytime after you say "I do," it is marital property.

An individual spouse may own marital property in his or her name alone. In many situations a spouse may, without the consent of the other spouse, dispose of his or her solely-owned, marital property without consequence. In some situations, however, what would otherwise be a legitimate and defendable transfer, may be undone by a divorce court or may bring with it (even years later) a valid claim for damages by the other spouse.

A couple may at anytime agree as to how certain property should be divided, either before or after the marriage. Pre- and post-nuptial agreements can be very flexible, very detailed, and very enforceable. A Pre-nuptial agreement is an agreement entered into by prospective spouses prior to marriage but in contemplation and consideration thereof; by it, the property rights of one or both of the prospective spouses are determined or are secured to one or both of them or their children. Post-nuptial agreements are made after marriage between couples still married; they take the form of separation agreements, property settlements in contemplation of a separation or divorce, or property settlements where there is no intention of the parties to separate. Both the pre- and post-nuptial agreements must, however, follow certain formalities. An inadequately crafted or executed pre-or post-nuptial agreement will be subject to very close scrutiny and sometimes a strong challenge in any divorce

Non-marital property can change forms and still retain its non-marital character as long as the ownership of the property is not put into a form of co-ownership with the other spouse. For example: you own a home before the marriage. That makes it non-marital property. When you sell the home, the money you receive in the sale is still your non-marital property. If you take the proceeds from the sale and buy a sports car, the sports car is your non-marital property. If you sell the sports car and put the proceeds from that sale into a joint checking account, you've probably converted the cash into marital property.

The process of defining property as being either marital or non-marital continues until a Judgment for Dissolution is entered into. The Judgment for Dissolution is the point in time where a judge signs off on the judgment and the case is finally concluded. A common mistake made by many, is that they think that property is non-marital if it is acquired after the filing of a divorce case, or after the parties separate. This is not true. Property, which has been acquired after your case has been filed, is still marital property. That continues to be true until the judge deems the couple officially divorced. For example: If you move out of your home and purchase a condo and fill it with your own furnishings and artwork, the condo and all its contents are still presumed to be marital property. If you play the lottery and win immediately after your case has been finalized, the winnings are yours and yours alone.

All of the aforementioned rules and definitions result only in presumptions, not conclusions. The court presumes property to be either marital or non-marital; and any and all presumptions may be rebutted by either party with the right kind of evidence.

GIFTS

As previously stated, property received as a gift is presumed to be non-marital. With the appropriate evidence and testimony though, the presumption can be overcome in court. Easily distinguishable examples though are the following: when someone from outside the marriage makes a gift to one spouse and gifts received by a spouse at a retirement party or from co-workers. Gifts that are received from relatives, however, can be very difficult to decipher. The following question is often asked: was it a gift to the individual (non-marital) or a gift to the couple (marital)?

The definition of gifts is not always that simple. For example, wedding gifts are usually thought to be given to the newly married couple, not to one spouse or the other, and are therefore usually considered marital property. Some wedding gifts, on the other hand, are given to one spouse only. Some are even given before the marriage, which deems them pre-marital (non-marital) property. The wedding rings themselves, in general terms, are considered gifts and are usually thought of as non-marital property.

PROPERTY PURCHASED IN CONTEMPLATION OF MARRIAGE

Sometimes a couple will buy a home right before their marriage, at times, even the day of the marriage just before the ceremony. Theoretically, such property should be viewed as non-marital because it was acquired before the marriage, but many courts will ignore the technicality and conclude that the home is, in reality, marital property. The cases depend on specific facts.

FACTORS AFFECTING PROPERTY DIVISION

It cannot be presumed that property will be divided 50/50 and many cases are resolved by the court or settled by the parties with 60/40 or 70/30 split and some even allocate all marital property to one spouse. The court looks to certain factors set out in the law when considering how to divide the marital property in equitable distribution. By law, the court is prohibited from considering marital misconduct in dividing both the property and debts. The property will still be divided fairly without acknowledging the damage caused by any harmful deeds such as a spouse having had several affairs and destroying the relationship.

FACTORS THE COURT CONSIDERS IN EQUITABLE DISTRIBUTION

Contribution

The court must consider the extent to which each party contributed "in the acquisition, preservation, or depreciation or appreciation in value, of the marital and non-marital property." It is reasonable to state that the party who brought in most of the income during the marriage should leave with most of the assets when the case is over. Every single case is determined by its own facts and circumstances. Courts take this very seriously and take everything into account. Decisions allocating fractions of percentages are not uncommon – 59.5% : 40.5% in one well-known case. Some attorneys have argued that if the parties have enough income to get by and have no real need, then all marital property should be divided strictly according to the proportionate contribution of each party. The court looks to more than just contribution alone; it is only but factor that courts consider in light of all the others.

Homemaker Contribution

The courts often view a marriage is as a "joint enterprise." They think of marriages like business partnerships. As in a lucrative business, they take in money, spend money, and keep themselves going. One of the partners (spouses) may go to work every day to bring in the money while the other partner stays home all day to keep the house, cook, and raise children. The court often sees the contributions of a homemaker as substantial and can be considered on the same level as with monetary contributions. Determination of the extent and value of such homemaking often becomes an important component of the forensic accounting engagement.

Homemaker contributions is not always a certainty in the division of marital property. In particular, cases when the there are no children. There have been several cases that have concluded that either little or no property was awarded when there are no children and when the homemaking essentially went undone. In some cases where the homemaking and child raising were shared equally, the homemaker contributions of each spouse tended to cancel one another out. There is no exact way of evaluating what "homemaker contribution" is worth because each case is judged on its own unique set of facts and circumstances. A frequent and important role of forensic accountants, however, is to identify and relate, in a quantitative way, such facts and circumstances.

Dissipation

Dissipation occurs when one spouse needlessly wastes property or money. The law applies itself to non-marital as well as marital property. Many spouses think that it's a better idea to spend their assets than to give their spouse a chance of receiving part of it. Dissipation claims are not limited to wasting money. The destruction and failure to maintain property also is considered as dissipation. Such things as homes falling into foreclosures, ruined photographs, and anything that may be left out to rust have all been found to be dissipation by some courts. Even such acts as failing to pay taxes on time has led some courts to conclude that the money needed to pay off the resulting interest and penalties was to be regarded as dissipation. Forensic accountants should be on the lookout for such events.

The court may use the final property award to offset the amount against the spending of the wasting spouse to compensate the wronged spouse when dissipation arises. For example, if, shortly before a divorce the spouse closed an investment account and used the money to buy a car for a "friend," the court would likely conclude that the money had been dissipated. The spouse would have to pay that amount back into the marital pie before it is divided. Pragmatically, the court typically applies an offset in the final property award.

Within the settlement struggles, a claim of dissipation can also be used as a weapon. Some spouses make outrageous claims that assets have been "dissipated" when, in fact, they've only been used in their ordinary daily lives. Alternatively, ordinary, day-to-day living expenses have, in come cases, been found to constitute dissipation.

A common example of a case is after the marriage had broken down; the husband had moved out of the house and rented an apartment. The wife made the argument that all of the rent money he paid had been dissipated and the judge ruled in her favor. Yet, in other cases, the expenditure of marital funds by one spouse for necessary, appropriate, and legitimate living expenses was not be counted as dissipation. Communication with the client attorney as to various legal strategies under consideration should provide the forensic accountant with direction as to which sort of economic evidence is required to support a particular strategy.

Value of Property Assigned

The word "assigned" refers to the value of the **non-marital** property assigned to each spouse. The court may find justice in awarding a disproportionate share of the marital assets to the other spouse if one spouse has significant non-marital assets. Also, the spouse with a sizeable non-marital estate may have to deal with a disproportionate share of the marital debt.

Duration of the Marriage

Consideration of the length and duration of the marriage serves two purposes. A long marriage generally operates as a multiplier of the homemaker contribution. Consideration of a short marriage generally would work to prevent the money hungry from marrying millionaires one day and divorcing them the next in an attempt to acquire a chunk of their wealth.

The homemaker contributions tend to carry a heavier weight in the court's allocation of property when one spouse may have sacrificed a lifetime career for the benefit of the children and home. This is especially true in marriages that are relatively long in length.

On the other hand, with marriages of relatively shorter length, the argument for the homemaker contribution is severely weakened. Usually there aren't any children and there has not been the opportunity to make much associating sacrifices and that much of a home. Several courts facing short-marriage cases will just assign to each party the property they brought to the marriage. An example is when, shortly after the marriage, one spouse sells a pre-marital home and rolls the proceeds over into the down-payment on a new house. The title is then put in the names of both spouses. That makes the house marital property. If a divorce follows soon thereafter, the first spouse may lose a great deal of that money and the other spouse may gain a lot just for being alive and married on the day of the closing. This is what the logic of the duration of marriage factor seeks to prevent. When duration of marriage is likely to be a factor in property apportionment, verification of property transaction dates becomes an important component of the forensic accounting engagement.

Relevant Economic Circumstances

The court has the power to allocate property to achieve substantial equity between the parties. The economic circumstances of each spouse must be considered in order to do so. A spouse may have a secure career and guaranteed future while another may be unemployed or unemployable. The less financially secure party is sometimes allocated more property by the courts as a way of affording them some additional security.

Prior Marriages

Though not an often occurrence, if a spouse receives child support or maintenance from a prior divorce, or if one party has additional responsibilities to children from a prior marriage, the court may consider that when dividing property in the present marriage.

Agreements

Prenuptial and post-nuptial agreements can be very flexible and very enforceable. Some agreements identify as non-marital property specific property that may or may not eventually be owned by one of the parties. Some agreements even go so far as to exclude all – that's right, ALL – property acquired during the marriage from being identified as "marital" and instead treat all property as the non-marital property of the acquiring party.

Situational Status

In the division of marital property, courts will also look to their own awards of custody, visitation, child support, and maintenance. Sometimes one party needs the house more than the other, or possibly a particular vehicle is more useful to one than the other. These issues are taken into consideration when dividing property.

Custody

In making property distributions, the court must take into account its custody award. To help compensate the added costs of caring for the children, sometimes a parent who is awarded custody will receive a larger share of the marital estate. The custodial parent is usually awarded the home as part of the division property. Many state laws contain specific provisions addressing this situation. Other provisions in the law allow the court the power to let the custodial parent stay in the home for a given time, such as until the children begin college, and then give the home to the non-custodial parent or sell it and divide the profits.

Maintenance

Courts like finality in divorce cases. They prefer not to see the feuding sides return a few years later in another dispute. The court sometimes makes a disproportionate property division that will prevent the need for maintenance. By doing so, the court eliminates the chance for something to go wrong in the future. Often enough, those required to pay maintenance fail to pay the correct amount, fail to pay on time, or fail to pay period. Recipients take actions to warrant an early termination of maintenance. New circumstances can occur to one of the party's that may warrant a modification, suspension, or termination of maintenance. A disproportionate property division and a denial of maintenance can remove these uncertainties. Under such circumstances, an accurate valuation of the aggregate property by a forensic accountant is especially important, since disproportionate distribution will turn an inaccurate valuation into an inequitable apportionment.

Future Income

In today's society, most marriages see both spouses working. It is no longer a common occurrence to witness a lifelong housewife. At most, some parents will put their careers on hold for a few years while children are in infancy. After that, they resume their place in the workforce. The difference in incomes becomes more obvious in higher income brackets.

A great gap in the incomes of the parties involved at the time of divorce may warrant a unequal division of property. Long term income trends are reviewed by the court when making such determinations. Unfortunately, a particularly good year for a spouse before the divorce may come back to hurt them when the court begins to divide property. The opposing counsel might argue that the spouse's recent income, in his last year, is the better measure of their ability to earn income. This is opposed to the previous years when they might have been still building their business, practice, career, and client base. The attorney might have to show the court that the last, good, year was merely a coincidence and a deviation from their usual annual income. Forensic accountants can provide valuable assistance in such situations by helping to identify factors that would support the contention that the particular year was a deviation (e.g., a one-time, non-recurring bonus based on a specific, unlikely to be repeated metric) or by performing comparative or averaging calculations that might demonstrate that the particular year in question was an aberration.

The future income component is not limited to long-term future income. Temporary unemployment has been used successfully to obtain a larger share of the marital estate; and some spouses have been suspected of arranging their own unemployment status at just the right time to maximize their share of the property division.

Taxes

Tax consequences of property distributions should be considered in any divorce. Forensic accountants are typically called upon to estimate these consequences. For example, it is too common for a spouse to be awarded stock or other investments instead of cash, only to later learn that to convert the stock to cash, they will have to pay taxes upwards of 50%.

Awards of maintenance and child support also are impacted by taxes. Significant tax considerations are present even when there is an agreement that the custodial parent will remain in the house until the children finish school, and is followed by the sale of the home.

MIXING MARITAL AND NON-MARITAL ASSETS

Determining what happens when marital and non-marital property is mixed is one of the more complicated issues in divorce law, affects almost every case, and is a great challenge to forensic accountants. Almost every case has some form of the problem.

Commingling of assets occurs when marital property is contributed to one spouse's non-marital asset, or vice versa. The character of the asset doesn't change, but the commingling creates a right of reimbursement or separation. For example, say a spouse had a bought a car before the marriage and at the time of the marriage there was a small balance due on the loan. If, after the marriage, marital assets such as a paycheck are used to pay off the car, marital assets have been contributed to a spouse's non-marital estate. The car remains the spouse's non-marital property, but the marital estate has a right to be reimbursed for the amount of the contribution.

Commingling also can occur when non-marital property is contributed to the marriage. The contributing non-marital estate has a right of reimbursement against the receiving marital estate, but the character of the receiving asset does not change from "marital" to "non-marital" just because of the transfer. Following on the example above, say after the wedding a minivan is purchased and financed in part with a loan. Later, a car you owned before the marriage (non-marital) is sold and proceeds from the sale (the cash from the sale of a non-marital asset is still non-marital property) are applied against the minivan loan balance. Non-marital assets (non-marital cash) have been contributed to the marital estate. The minivan doesn't become partly non-marital. Instead, it remains marital property and there exists a right of reimbursement against the marital estate.

Rights of reimbursement are not guaranteed in court. The economic analysis will not reach too far back in time, either. In the aforementioned examples involving cars, remember that the value of the car depreciates and, before long, the asset would be worth little or nothing and all rights of reimbursement would probably be extinguished.

Commingling: "Transmutation"

Transmutation refers to the situation where non-marital property is changed into marital property during a marriage. Various state laws provide that martial property can be transmuted into non-marital property in a number of ways.

An example of transmutation is when a spouse closed on a house just before the marriage and then after the marriage both spouses lived in the house and only the first spouse (the purchaser) made all the mortgage payments. Although the house was purchased prior to the marriage, only a small portion of it may be non-marital. If the mortgage payments,were made with marital property funds, as these marital funds are applied to a non-marital asset, the asset slowly takes on a marital character with each monthly payment. In such circumstances, the forensic accountant may be called upon to identify the sources of funds for some specific number of mortgage payments. Complications rapidly arise when the funds themselves are co-mingled.

RETIREMENT INVESTMENTS (401(K)S), AND IRA'S

Pension Benefits

During the course of a marriage, any pension benefits earned, or even any contributions made, are usually considered to be marital property; therefore they are susceptible to apportionment in the case of a divorce. Pension benefits that are part of the marital portion is commonly divided between spouses in one of two ways. The first way is known as "the offset method." Here, the spouse that does not hold the pension receives an amount equal to his or her percentage share of the current value of the marital portion of the asset. The second way to divide the marital portion of a pension is by using a Qualified Domestic Relations Order, also known as QDRO. Under a QDRO, a divorce judge gives the institution that handles the pension a set of instructions. The instructions detail how much each party will receive of the pension upon retirement.

First, the value of the marital portion of the pension must be determined. This will determine how much money each spouse will be paid, making it the most important part of the divisions. The segregation method, subtraction method, and the coverture method are the three methods forensic accountants typically use to value pensions. Each method arrives at different values because different information to value the pension shares are used.

Social Security

Benefits received from Social Security are usually not split between spouses in the case of a divorce. "The Federal statute, consistent with its remedial purpose, provides for the various contingencies of life, including the dissolution of marriage. Since the statute itself provides for an equitable distribution of its benefits to dependents, spouses, divorced spouses, and other family members in the event certain contingencies occur, we will not disturb the statutory scheme by suggesting any award of any part of the actual social security retirement benefits to which respondent may be entitled upon his reaching retirement age."

SAVING THE HOUSE: INJUNCTIONS AGAINST FORECLOSURE

Problems often arise in the case of a marital residence. One example is when a spouse stops paying the bills which can lead to foreclosure and the eventual sale of the marital residence. The divorce court can sometimes force one spouse or the other to make the payments. A prudent approach is often to use the forensic accountant to monitor mortgage payments and check tax records to uncover such actions as early as possible.

CONCLUSION

Once assets are classified as "marital" or "non-marital," the court then can equitably divide and distribute the marital property between the parties. An equitable division may not necessarily be an equal division. As this paper illustrates, division of property in the martial framework lends itself to inherent problems that depend on each individual circumstance.

CHAPTER 9

Determining Economic Income for Divorce Purposes when the Spouse Owns a Closely Held Business[*]

Bruce L. Richman

INTRODUCTION

In valuing a closely held business, one key component is the normalizing of the earning stream to be used. Based on documents the valuator receives, discussions with management, performance of a site visit, and independent research, the business valuator determines what, if any, adjustments need to be made to the original financial statements provided. This process is known as "normalizing" the financial statements. Some of the items that the business valuator looks for are: the owner's discretionary expenses, which are sometimes referred to as "perks;" related party transactions that do not reflect market rates, such as the company leasing space from a building that is owned by the owner of the company at above-market rates; non-operating assets that do not relate to the operations of the business; non-recurring items; and compensation to the owner that does not reflect market rates; among other items. Based on the analysis that the business valuator performs, he/her is usually in a good position to continue the discovery process in order to fully develop the benefits that the owner of the closely held business receives as an owner.

---

[*] Selected excerpts from "Eye on Business: Determining the True Income of an Entrepreneur" by Bruce L. Richman, published in *Family Advocate*, Vol. 23, No. 2, Fall 2000, a publication of the American Bar Association. Reprinted with permission. Additional material adapted from *JK Lasser Pro: Guide to Tax and Financial Issues in Divorce* by Bruce L. Richman, © 2000, John Wiley & Sons.

Bruce L. Richman CPA/ABV, CVA, CDP, Managing Director Business Valuation and Divorce Consulting Services, Trenwith Valuation, LLC, an affiliate company of BDO Seidman, LLP, Chicago, IL.

STORY OF "RAIDS"

In most divorce cases where maintenance or child support is involved, the issue of your spouse's true income becomes important. This is usually even more of an issue when a spouse is an owner of his/her own business. Experience has shown that in such situations it is important to verify that his/her salary as reported on his W-2 is in fact his/her true income. It is not uncommon that when the business owner spouse is faced with a divorce, their income along with the value of the business, mysteriously goes down. The spouse will usually claim that the economy is bad and the business is having financial problems. In the divorce community this situation is usually referred to as having the case of "RAIDS" – Recently Acquired Income Deficiency Syndrome. This is most common for those spouses who are the owners of their own businesses. Businesses that were very profitable suddenly go into total decline during the divorce. It is so amazing the correlation between the date of divorce and the decline of the Roman Empire. In most cases one can trace the direct correlation between the decline in earnings of the business and the shareholder spouse and the date of the divorce proceedings.

The following graph clearly demonstrates the date of the divorce proceeding.

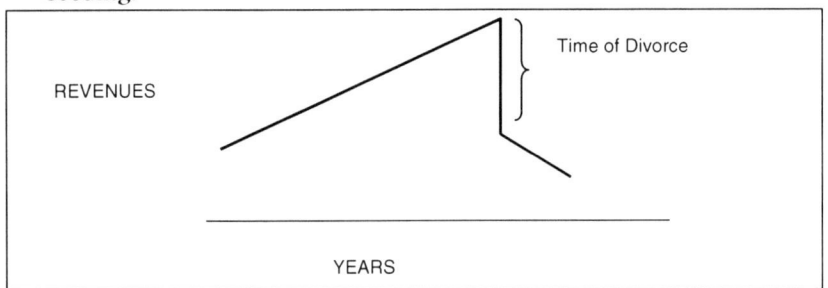

Finding the Expert

Finding a business valuator who also has the skills of a forensic accountant can be a valuable member of the divorce team in situations like this. They are used to having to dig into the depths of the corporate books to develop the normalized earnings of the business that they are valuing. In these cases the business valuator serves two purposes, one is to value the business and the second is to develop the economic benefits that the owner(s) receive from the business. The valuation expert / financial divorce consultant, if used properly, will play an important role in assisting the attorney in the discovery phase of the divorce case. The valuator/divorce consultant can assist the attorney in developing proper discovery requests, such as documents to ask for in a notice to produce; assist in developing questions for the deposition of the spouse and other management personnel (it is also very beneficial to have the expert attend the deposition to assist the attorney with follow up questions and interpret certain responses of the person giving the deposition); assist in the development of questions for interrogatories; and interpret financial records that are produced. Additionally, the expert should be prepared to assist the attorney in determining what drives the value of the business, and the controls the owner spouse has over the business. Also, as part of the process the divorce consultant should interview not only the opposing spouse, assuming their attorney would allow it, but to also interview the client. During the interview of your client, assuming he/she is the non-propertied spouse, though she/he may feel she/he does not know anything, in fact she may be a wealth of information. The expert should be asking about the family's life style, does the spouse use the corporate credit card when they go out, how are airline tickets paid for, does he or she bring household items home from the business, and other similar inquires. The expert will try to get an understanding on how the family lived and this may lead to important questions to ask the spouse in his/her deposition or in interrogatories. Understanding the standard of living during the marriage will assist the expert in developing his/her theory for the spouse's true economic income.

The expert will also play a very important part at the beginning of the process in assisting the attorney with what documents will be needed for his/her analysis. The expert can assist in developing a notice to produce to the other spouse as well as riders to be attached to subpoenas to banks, brokerage firms, related companies, vendors, etc.

Presentation of Findings

Presentation of the conclusions is an important step in the process as well. Summarizing your findings so that a trier of fact can reach the same conclusions you are pursuing is critical. Thus, one should summarize their findings in a straightforward format and than have footnotes and supporting exhibits to give detail supporting the individual items shown on the conclusion exhibit. Note that the exhibits produced in this analysis should tie back into the exhibits used for normalizing the earnings in the valuation of the related closely held business. Remember that the two exercises can be done in conjunction with each other. The following is an example of an exhibit used in summarizing one's True Economic Income.

Marriage of Brite
Case No 01 D 0001

Calculation of Dr. Joe Brite
ECONOMIC BENEFITS from
White Teeth Dental Practice
Year Ended December 31, 2002

W-2 WAGES:		
White Teeth Dental Practice		$105,000
CASH REVENUES NOT REPORTED BY THE PRACTICE		
AND TAKEN OUT BY OWNER - DR. BRITE (a safe is maintained at the Brite residence where the cash is stored for personal use)		$40,000
PERSONAL EXPENSES PAID BY WHITE TEETH DENTAL PRACTICE		
Mr. Brite's Jaguar lease payments	$14,500	
Mrs. Brite's Mercedes lease payments	11,000	
Personal auto repairs	250	
Personal auto insurance	3,000	
Personal life insurance	2,500	
Professional fees related to divorce	27,500	
Personal credit card payments	15,000	
Vacation home expenses	500	
Payment of house account at local liquor store	250	
Flowers for Mr. Brite's girlfriend, Tia	200	
Personal travel paid by White Tooth Dental	9,500	
Payments to Tia (which are funneled to her by putting her on the payroll as a "ghost employee"	21,500	
Above market rent on dental facility (Mr. Brite personally owns building)	10,000	
Excess/premium paid on dental materials purchased from XYZ which is owned by Mr. Brite's brother, Ned (XYZ maintains a slush account for Mr. Brite to use for personal expenditures)	15,000	
Salaries paid to Brite's children (ages 8 and 10)	20,000	
Cellular phone and pagers	500	
Personal income taxes paid by White Teeth	72,000	
		$223,200
DISTRIBUTIONS FROM ABC (ABC is a S-Corporation) amount shown on Dr. Brite's Form K-1 and on Federal Form 1120		$148,000
TOTAL ECONOMIC BENEFITS		$516,200
Income Taxes Withheld per W-2[1]		
Federal income tax withheld	$14,540	
Social Security withheld	4,500	
Medicare withheld	1,520	
Illinois income tax withheld	2,950	
Income Tax Withheld		$23,510
Income Tax Payments		
Estimated Federal income tax	$60,000	
Estimated State income tax	10,000	
Total Tax Payments		$70,000
Total Taxes		-$93,510
NET ECONOMIC BENEFITS FOR Dr. Brite from White Teeth Dental Practice		$422,690

[1] Rather than use what was withheld, using the actual amount paid per the Doctor's personal Federal and State income tax return might be more appropriate if available. Some may also argue that you should input the income tax relating to the perks - but the counter argument is that no actual tax is currently being paid on this economic income.

As can be seen on the exhibit, the spouse's annual W-2 is only the beginning when dealing with a closely held company. This chapter will provide you with samples of places to look and items to address in the never-ending saga of the true income of the owner of a privately held business. The purpose of the following is to give you an understanding of the issues and a sample of the things to look for. It is not exhaustive and each case will have its own specific issues to address. Before necessarily looking at the specifics of the "perks" from the business, which may be difficult to find without costly discovery, one may first start by showing that perks in the general scheme of things do exist. Once proven, the spouse may come clean and shortcut the process and save family funds that would have been used in the investigation. So, the next step is to look at some methods that can be used to determine that the spouse is not showing all of his/her true economic income. One method that is commonly used is a Net Worth Analysis.

Net Worth Analysis

As indicated above, one method used to determine that the spouse is not disclosing his/her true economic income is a net worth analysis. This may be a good place to start, especially if funds are limited and needed records have not been produced. In this analysis, you will compare the net worth of the spouse at two specific periods of time. Net worth of an individual is simply the addition of all assets subtracted by all liabilities of the individual. This same concept can also be applied at the business level. In doing this analysis you need to remember that the assets need to be valued at cost. Basically, you will compare the change in net worth [this is determined by looking at the net worth of the estate "at COST" at the beginning of the selected period and comparing it to the net worth "at COST" at the current period] and then add your living expenses for each year and subtract your known income for each of those years. There are some flaws in this method that the valuator should be aware of (a) the net worth at the beginning of the period that you are comparing to may be understated due to hidden assets or (b) the individual may have obtained additional assets subsequent to the date of comparison which may not have been detected by the valuator or even visible to the parties. The concept is summarized as follows:

Start with:	Change in the spouse's Net Worth
Plus:	Total expenses paid out or incurred
Subtract:	Sources of Income
The net amount will indicate the amount of unknown income	

If the change in the net worth is greater than that income which is reported on the spouse's affidavit, the difference may represent unreported income. Another item one may also have to consider in the calculation above is any gifts received or made and inheritances received during the period of analysis. It is interesting to note that the IRS also uses this net worth method to reconstruct income for taxpayers who are suspected of tax fraud or just an underreporting of income. The sources of information can come from the federal income tax returns, loan applications, and the expense affidavit filed in your case. Under this analysis, the expense affidavits play an important part, especially when a spouse has signed under oath the income and expense disclosure as being true and accurate. Lying or misrepresenting facts on an income and expense affidavit can come back to bite the spouse under this analysis. For example if the spouse is down-playing the life style, it will likely be revealed as an unexplained variance in the use of the family's income, or in other words, a possible claim of dissipation.

LIFE STYLE ANALYSIS

The expense affidavit is also used in a similar method where you compare the party's living expenses as identified on the expense affidavit to the income being reported. While the expense affidavit is a starting point, you will need to also investigate other life style expenses that may not be on the expense affidavit. These will come into play in discussions with each of the spouses and a review of the actual spending by the parties and the review of actual invoices. Many a client has surprised an unsuspecting spouse who denied having unreported cash or using cash, when the other spouse produced numerous receipts for thousands of dollars stamped paid in cash and showed that the merchandise was shipped to their residence. It is amazing how one can have twice as much in expenses than the income they are generating without reducing one's net assets.

Other Analyses

Also tied into the above methods, is to review the various bank accounts of the individuals. You can simply add up the cash expenditures, plus the cash balance less the identified sources of cash; the difference would indicate unknown source of cash to investigate further. Another simple initial way to compute the party's cash flow is to review the individual income tax returns and tie this to the lifestyle analysis and then question the make up of the variances that appear.

This leads us to the basis of the process which is obtaining the proper documentation to perform one's analysis and supporting of the conclusions reached.

DOCUMENTATION

Information to begin the process will come from your discovery process and the valuators site visit and interview with management or through depositions and interrogatories. Thus, the importance of a site visit and management interview cannot be minimized. Whether or not you are engaged by the propertied or non-propertied spouse you should perform a site visit of the company and its operations. A site visit is a key element of the appraisal process that should not be ignored. Direct observation of assets that do not show up on the books of the company or corporate assets being used by the owner spouse is another factor to consider. However, even though the spouse may be the owner of the company, he/she may not have an active role in running the closely held business. This limited role in the management of the company may reduce the ability of the owner spouse to use the company's assets for his/her personal use. On the other hand, the more control the owner spouse has in the operations of the closely held business, the more likely the need to be cautious and a more thorough forensic examination of the potential perks is indicated. Another item to look for during the site visit is the extent of the company's internal controls and how cash transactions are being handled and whether or not all transactions are properly recorded, or at least the procedures are in place to ensure this. Find out who controls these areas and functions and talk with them or depose them if need be.

Basic documents such as personal and business Credit Reports, bank statements, cancelled checks (front and back), deposit slip details, debit and credit memos, check registers, signature cards, monthly credit card statements, applications for credit cards or checking accounts, loan applications, etc. should be requested. This is a good time to mention that requesting a copy of both spouses credit report can sometimes yield some reveling information. It can provide you with bank accounts, credit cards and other loans you may not have been aware of. A number of credit reports also provide information as to when accounts were opened; highest levels of amount owed; when loans were paid off; as well as the current balance of credit cards and loans. This may also lead the forensic accountant / divorce financial consultant to question refinance proceeds that may show up on the credit report that did not show up on any bank account statements that have been disclosed.

With respect to the business, you will want to obtain items such as: detailed general ledgers; cash disbursement journals; payroll records; copies of contracts for services; lease agreements; bank statements; deposit slips; credit card statements; loan files; any brokerage statements; telephone records; etc. This is where the spouse of the company owner can be useful in reviewing and highlighting the personal nature of certain expenditures. This than can be followed up with direct questioning of the spouse and others through the use of specific questions drafted for a deposition of these individuals or the development of questions for interrogatories.

Also, obtaining the individual's gift tax returns may be helpful in identifying assets that have been transferred.

Another thing worthwhile in discovery might be to have counsel do a search, (usually in the state or states that the spouse lives or does business) for those entities incorporated in their name or the name of other hidden affiliates or relatives. Also remember to obtain tax returns for several years. Not only will you want to cross check the assets on the asset disclosure statements of the spouse with those showing income on the tax returns, you will also want to track the sources of income that may have changed from one year to the next. For example, if the past three years the couple reported on the joint federal individual income tax return dividends from stocks held at *Brokerage A* and then for the year of the divorce no dividends show up on the Schedule B of the Federal Individual income tax return, this would lead you to investigate the disappearance of this brokerage account. Also be aware of non-taxable income, such as tax-exempt interest, which is also shown on the tax return.

The following is a list of suggested items that might be included in your notice to produce.

- Personal Records
  1. Personal Income Tax Returns – 5 years;
  2. Phone records – monthly detail of phone statements for both regular phone and the spouse's cell phone
  3. Credit reports;
  4. Bank statements;
  5. Cancelled checks (front & back);
  6. Deposit slip details;
  7. Debit and credit Memos;
  8. Check registers;
  9. Monthly credit card statements;
  10. Credit card applications;
  11. Loan applications;
  12. Personal financial statements;
  13. K-1's for all Partnerships and Subchapter S Corporations;
  14. Gift Tax Returns to identify transferred assets;
  15. All paid bills and receipts;
  16. Copies of each security buy/sell advice and broker's monthly transaction statements;
  17. Copies of any taxing authority's revenue agent's reports;
  18. Copies of automobile, boat or plane registrations owned individually or by the business;
  19. Details of all purchases and sales of real estate
  20. Stock options; and,
  21. Frequent flyer statements from all airlines and statements from hotel programs and restaurant frequent dining programs.

- Business Records

    1. Completed books of original entry

        a. Cash Receipts Journal;

        b. Cash Disbursements Journal;

        c. General Ledger;

        d. Payroll Journal;

        e. Sales Journal;

        f. Petty Cash Journal; and,

        g. Purchase Journal.

    2. Subsidiary Ledgers

        a. Accounts Receivable Ledger (billed & unbilled); also request an aging of accounts receivable.

        b. Accounts Payable Ledgers; also request an aging of the accounts payables.

        c. Payroll Ledger;

        d. Perpetual Inventory Records;

        e. Fixed Asset work papers and depreciation lapse schedules;

    3. Copies of all financial statements, including footnotes, whether interim or year-end, prepared internally and/or audited, including all work papers prepared by the accountants supporting the financial statements.

    4. Copies of any financial information prepared for bank loans or for obtaining credit. As a matter of course, subpoenas should be issued to all financial institutions, which provide credit to the business. Make sure you get the complete credit file! It is not uncommon for the credit department of the bank to prepare a complete financial analysis of the company and the owning spouse.

    5. Copies of all Income Tax Returns, including all schedules and attachments and any accountant's work papers used to pre-

pare such tax returns. Copies of all tax notices and taxing authority revenue agent's reports.

6. All financial records supporting the entries made in the company's books, including but not limited to:

   a. Cancelled checks, bank statements and deposit slips; it may be important to see if they deposit cash. This will show up on the deposit slips. Also, if you get copies of the checks that were deposited you may get a lead as to those customer checks that are missing but show up in their account receivables having been paid.

   b. Detailed schedules prepared from all receivables, payables and inventories;

   c. All paid bills and receipts, including applicable charge card statements and receipts. In a closely held business you may request this for all credit cards issued, not just the owner spouse, as others may have access to credit cards for the benefit of the owner spouse.

   d. Notes, mortgages and other evidences of indebtedness;

   e. Property leases for both real and personal property;

   f. Copies of all depreciation lapse schedules;

   g. Copies of all compensation agreements;

   h. Copies of all Form 1099;a and W-2's issued;

   i. Copies of any employment contracts entered into;

   j. Copies of any budgets or projections;

   k. Buy-Sell Agreements; and

   l. Brokerage Statements.

- Miscellaneous Documents:

   1. List of directors and officers and their titles;

   2. Description and history of the company;

   3. Corporate Minute Book and stock transfer records;

   4. Schedule of states were qualified to do business;

   5. Organization chart;

6. List of major competitors, largest customers and sales volume to each;

7. List of shareholders or partners with number of shares owned by each;

8. Marketing literature;

9. List of main suppliers and customers; and

10. Copies of any appraisals of the business, property, real estate, etc.

Once the documents have been obtained and the forensic work performed, one may find many economic benefits received by the owner spouse and his/her family from the closely held business.

Economic Benefits Received from the Company

Some of the more straightforward items that are typical benefits, perks, or additional economic income to the owner are: automobile usage and personal use of the credit cards that are paid for by the company. In looking at the automobile you need to follow up with the related expenses such as gas, insurance, maintenance and parking expenses. Identifying the true nature of the spouse's job and the perks provided to other non-related employees can down play the argument of "business need." If the spouse only uses the company car, remember that driving to work is not a business need. Also, just because the company writes the expense off on the corporate tax return does not make it a business expense. Do not accept the old statement of: "the company was recently audited by the IRS and there was no changes" to mean no personal expenses went through the company. The type of audit conducted and the IRS agent performing the audit make a big difference on whether they even address the issue of personal items, or have even done the appropriate investigation to identify those personal expenses written off by the company or unreported income by the company and owner spouse. Simply put, the fact that the company had an IRS audit does not support, in and of itself, the spouse's assertion that no personal items went through the company, nor should it stop you from doing a proper and thorough analysis. Also review the balance sheet, depreciation lapse schedule and the M-1 adjustments to determine if the company owns personal autos, leases them, or just pays the cost of them directly for the benefit of the owner spouse and his/her family.

Corporate Credit Cards / Cash Disbursement Journal

In reviewing the cash disbursement journal you should be able to identify which credit cards that the company is paying for. It will be also important to identify all people who have credit cards that are paid for by the company and the relationship they have to the owner spouse. In an attempt to hide the personal use of the credit cards, the owner spouse may have other employees of the company charge items on their behalf so it wouldn't show up on the credit card of the owner spouse even though the company is still paying for it. Look at all credit card statements and raise the issue during the site visit and management interview. Tie this also with the employee expense reimbursement forms or whatever they file to get reimbursed for expenses they pay for. This may be a way the spouse gets to pay back a straw person or even directly himself. Again, just because they use an employee business expense reimbursement form doesn't automatically make it a business expense.

As you go through the cash disbursement journal or cancelled checks, identify those payments directly to the spouse, as there may be non-payroll checks that are being cashed for cash. Additionally, look at the back of the checks as they may show the deposit into accounts that you are not aware of. Additionally, looking at the back of the checks may also indicate to you who actually cashed the checks, which may be a different person or vendor than was recorded on the books of the company. The review of the payroll records may also indicate payments to relatives, friends or paramours that do not even work at the company. You may also need to look for fictitious employees by comparing payroll records to health insurance policies (the business owner will not usually bother to insure a phantom employee) or other records. You may also notice the loss of key employees who are either aware of the activities of the owner spouse or may have actually been involved in helping the spouse obtain the various perks. These former employees may be great people to talk to, especially if they did not leave on good terms.

In getting a picture as to where the owner spouse may be doing business or have transplanted assets, look at his/her frequent flyer statements and hotel points programs. This may lead you to frequent destinations at which the owner spouse spends a significant amount of time, which may also lead to non-business activities paid for by the business. This can also be followed up with a review of telephone records to locate numbers that are constantly used, which can lead to paramours or even clients that do not show on the books of the company.

Common Sizing the Financials

In reviewing the detail expenses of the company for the past several years and common sizing them, one can look for unusual increases or trends in a particular expense category that will require further investigation. Common sizing is taking each expense as a percentage of revenues. For example: Property taxes that had been 1.2% of revenues for four years straight and then in the last year increased to 2.5% would raise a question as to why. After further investigation, including the review of the real estate tax bills and discussions with the controller of the company, it may be determined that the owner spouse had acquired a condo for a paramour and the expenses were paid for by the company. Increases in the repairs & maintenance account or capitalized leasehold improvements when you are aware of no changes at the company's facilities, can lead to either activities at the spouses personal residence being paid for by the company or even a condo or house which you were not aware of that the spouse had. In connection with performing a trend analysis and common sizing the company's expenses, it may be worthwhile to benchmark the company's common sized expenses and financial ratios against similar type of companies. This can be done not only at the individual expense item level but also using key financial ratios that may lead to further investigation.

Depreciation Lapse Schedules

The depreciation lapse schedules are the company's detail depreciation schedules that are usually maintained by the company or its outside accountants. This is usually a more detailed schedule than what you may find as part of the corporate income tax return. This may also lead to the discovery of unplanned remodeling, upgrading and replacement of corporate facilities. This is a subtle way of using profits / funds that may have ordinarily been paid out to the owner spouse, thus in essence a reinvestment by the spouse into the business. A key is to talk to the company's controller, bookkeeper, or secretary/office manager. They may unknowingly provide you with the information that is needed. Also be aware of capital assets that are being expensed and thus may not show up on the depreciation schedules. This can be accomplished by keeping a keen eye during the site visit and compare what you have seen with what is on the depreciation lapse schedules or elsewhere on the balance sheet.

Insurance Policies

Detail review of the insurance policies that the company pays for can indicate payments for the spouse's home, car or life insurance policies that are not business related. A detailed review of the insurance policies may also indicate assets that you were not aware of as well. For example, the property and casualty policy may show an automobile driven by the owner spouse's significant other or a side condo being maintained by the company. Life insurance policies paid for by the company should be reviewed as to who the beneficiaries are as well as the insured. Sometimes over looked hidden asset may be a significant cash surrender value tied to an insurance policy or policy tied to an annuity, which may produce a significant earning stream at a later date. The current premium on these policies may be considered as additional economic benefit to the owner spouse.

Deferred Comp and Direct Pays

Be careful to review forms of deferred compensation arrangements, such as the use of phantom stock and stock appreciation rights that may not show up as current income. Tied into this is a review of the company's pension plan(s) for unusual or extraordinary payments credited to the owner spouse's account. This may be another way to move the spouse's income into another year, but still is a form of economic income for the current year.

Another source of a perk is for house accounts or direct pays. The company may have house accounts at a florist, liquor store or travel agency. The subpoenaing of these records and deposition of individuals of these businesses may also lead to extensive personal spending by the company on behalf of the owner, and possibly other indications as well. For example, the company may have a house account with a local florist, however, after subpoenaing the records of this vendor the routing sheets show that the flowers were not delivered to the office but rather the paramour of the owner spouse. Reviewing the purchase orders and receipts of house accounts at an office supply or warehouse supply store may indicate items being delivered to the personal residence of the owner spouse and not to the company. This document may also have a detail as to what was purchased which may indicate the personal nature of the item.

Loans

The obtaining of shareholder loans can be a disguise of income. This can be a way of providing funds to the spouse without including it on his W-2 as wages. Additionally, the sudden paying off of previous loans made to the company by the spouse may also be a way of changing the characteristic of funds obtained by the spouse. Regardless of what it may be called, this is another source of economic benefit to the spouse. Look for trends. Has the company ever borrowed money from the owners in the past or if there had been loans from shareholders on the books has the company paid down shareholder loans in the past or even interest? Compare these payments with other related items, such as, has shareholder/officers salaries gone down but shareholder loans are now being paid off? Remember that loans to the company may be a marital asset. Review the balance sheet of the company. Compare the shareholder loan activity with other owners in the company. Remember when dealing with an S-Corporation, the payment by the company to its shareholders relating to a loan repayment if correctly prepared will show up on the shareholder's Form K-1. Additionally, cash and property distributions should be shown on the shareholder's Form K-1 as well. If not shown on the K-1's, then review the detail general ledger and be careful to review the various classifications that the company may have used. Misclassification is often used to disguise the true nature of distributions.

Related Party Transactions

We must also not forget to investigate financial arrangements between the business and a related party to the owner spouse. For example, the building is being leased from a parent of the spouse and the rent is above current market rents. Also, look for gifts in that the parents after collecting the rent may be turning over the net profits to the spouse as a gift. In looking at proper rents, have the real estate appraiser address this issue as part of their work in determining the fair market value of the property.

You should also be aware of the concept of "parking profits" with friends. The business may have a venture relationship where it is not formally written in the agreement but there is an unwritten understanding that a share of the profits from the vendor "friends" would be given back to the owner spouse. One needs to look out for changes in customers and vendors and be aware of how the company conducts its business. Be aware of sudden shifts in cost of goods sold without increases being passed on to the customer or sudden changes in customers or suppliers. Also, look for significant purchases of inventory at year-end where the owner can possibly understate profits until after the divorce. An example of this is a case where the owner spouse would be paying significant commissions and bonuses to a member of his management team and after further investigation it was found that the manager had bought a boat which the owner spouse just happens to have the right to use at his leisure. On the other hand, you may need a compensation study/compensation expert to show that proper compensation was paid out to the shareholder spouse and the profits were just not reinvested or left inside the company.

Another way to look at unreported economic income is to review the personal payments of common expected payments of the household. For example, in a review of personal records you would expect to see payments to utility companies, auto and home insurance, real estate taxes, etc. An absence of these payments will lead you to ask how and by who where paying these expenses. A review of a sample of the company's utility bills might also direct you to other economic benefits to the owner spouse. If the family is known for constantly entertaining and traveling but no expenses show up on a review of the personal records, this is a good indication that they may be paid through the business and further investigation is warranted.

Assistance

Most business owners will need assistance with "RAIDS," thus a review of invoices from professionals to determine whether services were performed with respect to the business or were personal related. Even more important, does the detail billing indicate any changes in business patterns, transfer of assets, ownership changes, or any other type of planning? It is not uncommon that an owner spouse's salary is decreased but their life style does not seem to change. This is because the company is now paying for the owner spouse's personal expenses.

The detail review of the entertainment and travel category on the financial statements always needs to be reviewed. Look for trends and the number of meals taken in any one particular day. Compare this pattern to those prior to the divorce proceedings. Another item will be the use of cell phones. Determine how many phones the company is actually paying for and whom are the numbers assigned to. Ask for the employee's expense reports. Look at how they are recorded on the books of the company; how they compare to industry standards; how they compare to others in the company and how they relate to the role that the owner spouse plays in the company.

The Search for Cash

Where the company is in the manufacturing business, a review of the scrap sales can lead to significant unreported cash. Talking with the shop foreman or former employees can help in this area. Discussion with the bookkeeper as to how this is recorded is also helpful. This might also lead to the issue of sales that are not recorded or "out the backdoor sales." Compare bank deposit slips to day sheets or other company reports that record company daily sales and collection activity. In medical and dental practices, compare the appointment book to the day sheets and ultimately back to the bank deposit slips.

Obviously those businesses that deal with cash make it easier for the owning spouse to take the cash and not report it. When dealing with businesses that are paid heavily in cash, extra analysis must be done. Review closely the accounts receivable ledgers and look for credits or adjustments. Follow these up to make sure that the entry to reduce one's accounts receivable was off set with a deposit to cash. Also, review the deposits into the bank account and see if the deposit slips only show checks being deposited and no cash. The deposit slips will show what was deposited in cash and how much was from checks. If the company gets paid only in checks, look at the detail deposits and see if you observe all clients checks being deposited. If not, but you see credits to the accounts receivable, look to confirm the payment on outstanding receivables with clients and obtain canceled checks from the customer to review whether and where the checks were either cashed or deposited. For example, the client may be diverting the payments received by a particular client into a separate bank account under the name of the company but never showing up on the books of the company. Additionally, for those clients you know pay cash, select a sample of those cash sales that are recorded on the books of the company and trace them to see if they appear on the deposit slip for that time period.

For business such a laundromat, restaurants, bars, fruit stands, etc. the receipt of cash is significant. Though difficult, there are also ways to determine the non-reporting of cash. For example, the owner spouse runs a laundromat. The divorce now hits and business drops off. Obtain the water bills for the past several years. First, compare the water usage for this period of time and look at the trend. Obviously if the water usage has gone up, the reduction of business may not be accurate or just a case of RAIDS. Further, obtain the make and model of the washing machines and determine the amount of water that is used by the machines per wash and ultimately you can determine an approximate amount of money that should have been earned by the amount of water usage. Remember this also has a direct relationship to the dryer usage as well. For those with restaurants, a simple comparison of the restaurant's deposits with cash register tapes and individual tickets may be revealing. With the new computerized registers, all of the activity is maintained and can be compared with the actual amounts being deposited. For example, in a small sub shop, obtain the records from their vendor that supplies their rolls. Here there should be a direct relationship to the bread usage and the revenues of the sub shop. For these types of businesses, look for expense/income relationships. Obtain statistical data and compare this to the ratios for your business. For example, for a restaurant, compare the COGS % for the industry to your restaurant and if the percentages are too high it may mean that they are recording all of the costs but not the revenue side.

Obtain a detailed credit report on the individual and the business. In reviewing the credit analysis of the particular individual, look for those debts that have been paid off or dates of payments toward these debts. After identifying these items look through the checking accounts to find the canceled checks that correspond with the payments. This can lead to either cash payments or missing accounts or payments by a controlling entity.

Bartering

Something that has become more common is the use of bartering. Look for signs of this by payments to bartering associations. Also, those customers that show purchase orders and the reduction in the customer's accounts receivable is made through a credit entry and recording into the sales journal without a deposit into the bank account. The items received in the bartering may all be used for personal use. For example, the company enters into a legitimate bartering association, however the items received in the bartering process may be golf clubs or other personal items. The value of this goes into the spouse's true economic income.

Lastly, review the company's assets for significant prepaid assets; prepayment of credit cards; or annuities that are part of insurance policies.

Be on the Lookout

Once we know personal expenses are paid by the company some things to be on the lookout for, as discussed above, include the following:

- Personal insurance expenses such as homeowner, boat, automobile, liability, disability, life and hospitalization insurance;
- Personal clothing, food, furniture, gifts, drugs, jewelry, liquor, flowers – look for house accounts;
- Personal telephone, electric, utility and cellular phone bills;
- Gardner, snow removal, repairs and maintenance expenses in personal residence or vacation homes.
- Personal entertainment expenses, theatre tickets, sporting events, club dues;
- Personal legal fees;
- Personal or family member's automobiles, including gas, insurance, maintenance and parking fees;
- Personal and vacation travel expenses;
- Personal maid, cleaning services, alarm and sprinkler systems for personal residence;
- Payment of salaries for "no show" family members or companion;
- Payment of rent for companion's apartment or secondary in town apartment;

- Payment of excess rent to owner if the spouse is the landlord of company;

- Personal barter transactions not recorded on the books;

- School tuition for children;

- Medical expenses not covered by insurance being reimbursed to owner by company paid insurance policy for expenses paid by the company.

The Partner

Don't forget that if the spouse has a partner, putting pressure on the partner or fellow shareholder may provide results, especially if he/she was not aware of the perks your spouse had been receiving. Or just the threat that you plan on subpoenaing the owner spouse's partners may be enough to have him/her cooperate enough not to involve the fellow shareholders. In some cases it may be that the spouse's partners are also receiving unreported benefits. It is not uncommon in such situations for the owner spouse to settle or to become more helpful in the discovery plan. Just the threat of IRS problems may be enough to get everyone to cooperate and put pressure on the owner spouse to settle. The fear of the IRS is amazing. As indicated above, another key is whether all partners and/or shareholders are treated equally.

In summary, for those situations where the spouse has partners and/or shareholders as part of the closely held business you will need to ask yourself:

1. Are all partners or shareholders being treated similarly?

2. Are profits being distributed or do you sense that profits are being unreasonably retained? Several points should be reviewed, including the company history for paying bonuses, declaration of dividends, present and future capital needs, expansion plans, etc. You may also need to obtain a compensation study to determine if there is reasonable compensation being paid from the company to the owner spouse.

3. Does the company have non-operating assets such as brokerage accounts or real estate holdings not necessary to the daily operations of the business but rather for the benefit of one shareholder?

4. Has the owner spouse received advances or repayment of outstanding shareholder loans, which will not appear on his W-2 or 1040, while other shareholders or owners have not been repaid? How do payments to the spouse compare to other owners?

5. As you go through the cash disbursements journal or cancelled checks, identify non-payroll checks (i.e. reimbursements) that have been cashed for cash. Examine the back of checks for new bank accounts or third-party endorsements.

6. Identify, locate and interview former key employees who may be knowledgeable about the owner's activities or have been involved in helping secure various perks.

7. On a spot check, pull copies of the microfish copies of the deposits and see if all of the customers' checks are being deposited. Look at the billing and accounts receivable to see if the collections show up as a deposit in the company's bank account. Any questions can be resolved by requesting a copy of the cancelled check from the customer and review the back of the check for the location of its deposit.

The Financial Cost

All the above analysis is fine and good, but there is a financial cost for this. Most financial/divorce accountants charge for their services and given the extent of the digging, the cost can become quite high. One needs to carefully analyze the expected cost of the exercise and weigh this against the anticipated benefits. This is sometime difficult to do because in many cases you may not have an idea as to the extent of the unreported income. It is important to point out to the client that there is no guarantee that even the most thorough investigation may turn up significant unreported income or economic benefits that the spouse of the closely held business may be receiving, or if there are such benefits that they exist to an extent that exceeds the cost of the exercise. One thing to do to continually monitor the process once the engagement begins. At different points into the examination, you, the attorney, and the client may determine that based on the level of work performed to date, they are comfortable that the benefits to be derived will not out weigh the economic benefits. Having said this, the economic benefits may be overshadowed by the principal issues the spouse wants to prove or demonstrate: the character of the spouse to the court or for other non-economic aspects of the case. Another thing that this process may also accomplish is to either confirm or calm the level of mistrust and animosity that may exist between the two spouses. It is usually this level of mistrust and bitterness toward each other that usually pushes one spouse to hire the forensic/divorce consultant to begin in the first place. The examination may also be needed for determining the value of the closely held business. Whatever the decision is, it should be made early on in the process to give the divorce consultant time to perform their services, have full use of the discovery process, and not delay the settlement process.

CONCLUSION

Looking beyond the W-2 is the key. However, to do so opens a door with nothing but the unknown beyond. Before you take on a full forensic examination of the company and personal records of the spouse for the development of one's true economic income, don't forget to weigh and communicate the cost of such a task versus the economic benefit the spouse may receive from such an exercise. As discussed above, alternative methods may be more economically advisable. Having said this, the best cure for the case of RAIDS is the presentation to the court of the true economic income of the spouse. It is also amazing how this disease usually becomes cured upon the finality of the divorce proceeding or the obligations under it.

During the process, remember also the golden rule of "don't kill the goose that laid the golden egg." How far to pursue your investigation while a settlement is sought, and how you communicate the results of your investigation into RAIDS is sometimes as important as to finding it and now knowing what the spouse's true economic income is. Also, make sure you understand that your examination may indicate that the spouse has possibly committed tax fraud, and the consequences of this can be serious. Also, understand how this may impact the spouse of the owner of the closely held company. Remember, the payment of significant tax, interest and penalties may also economically impact both spouses, even if one ends up qualifying as an innocent spouse under IRC Section 6015.

CHAPTER 10

Selection of Business Valuation Experts in a Divorce: The Attorney Perspective

Paul H. Townsend and Alison C. Leslie

This chapter shall give guidance to attorneys as to how to choose the correct expert to utilize in the valuation of a business. It also, however, provides forensic accountants and other financial professionals with insight into some important factors that divorce attorneys consider in assisting the client with the business valuator selection. Selecting a business valuation expert in a divorce case is not as easy as it may seem. There are many practical considerations to utilize when choosing the right business evaluator. The expert who takes too long or costs too much money in relation to the asset may not only cost the client money that is not justified (and in most divorce cases the client can not afford), but may also cost the client the case. If that is not bad enough, the wrong expert can make a client question his or her attorney's judgment which then can literally cost that attorney the client when that client goes to another attorney or worse still when the client does not think that the attorney is capable of moving forward in the case. The right expert can make all the difference.

INTRODUCTION

The typical process of making an equitable distribution of the assets acquired during the marriage requires the Trial Court to initially identify all marital property. Next, the Court is required to value all marital property. Finally, the Court will make determinations as to the equitable distribution of the assets and order monetary awards where appropriate. Expert witness testimony is frequently used in this process to assist the Court in the identification and valuation of property.

Paul H. Townsend, Esq., partner, Cutler, Simeone, Townsend, Tomaio & Newmark, LLC, Morristown, NJ..

Alison C. Leslie, Esq., Cutler, Simeone, Townsend, Tomaio & Newmark, LLC, Morristown, NJ.

Businesses have emerged as one of the most difficult types of asset to value for divorce purposes. Forensic accountants have emerged as the key players in divorce litigation; whether they are testifying in the Trial Court, or assisting the parties and their attorneys in settlement negotiations.

CASE LAW

In the course of divorce litigation where one or both parties are owners of a business, the valuation of the business may be one of the most important aspects of the case. Certainly, other than alimony, it is usually the largest money issue in the case. The valuation of a business is not an exact science and is often a battle of experts. There is no right answer. See *Balsamides v. Perle*, 313 *N.J. Super.* 7, 34) (Wecker, J., concurring); *Balsamides v. Protameen Chemicals, Inc.*, 160 *N.J.* 352 (1999).

In his concurrence, Judge Wecker stated:

> In the final analysis, the outcome of each case is usually a compromise, with the Court often finding a value somewhere between the valuations sought by [one party] and [a] higher appraisal sought by the [other]. Since the facts of each case will determine the outcome, it is worth noting that case law is usually available to support any position regarding valuation of an interest in a closely held business. *Id* at 34.

The Trial Court must carefully weigh the facts presented through business valuations and testimony in creating a decision. A trial court is free to accept or reject the testimony of either expert and need not adopt the opinion of either expert in its entirety. *Carey v. Lovett*, 132 *N.J.* 44, 64 (1993). A business valuator must carefully analyze a business on a case-by-case basis, with sensitivity and adjustment for the particular circumstances and the flexibility to deal with extraordinary circumstances. See *John R. MacKay, II, 2* New Jersey Business Corporations '14-6(d) (1) (2d ed. 1996).

In order for the expert to analyze and appraise the business, there must be detailed information provided to the experts through discovery. *Esposito v. Esposito*, 158 *N.J. Super.*, 285, 294 (App. Div. 1978). From an examination of the books, an expert may then be able to determine the capital structure, net worth, and financial ratios customarily regarded as significant in determining the soundness of a business enterprise, *Lavene v. Lavene*, 148 N.J. Super., 267, 275 (App. Div. 1977).

In the *Lavene* case, the Defendant-Husband was a 43% owner of a corporation, which had a book value of $143,000.00; $98,000.00 of which was allocated on the books to goodwill. The Defendant-Husband has personally guaranteed $22,000.00 worth of corporate notes. The Trial Court deducted the $98,000.00 of goodwill from the $143,000.00 book value to arrive at a value for the corporation of $45,000.00. The Trial Court then apportioned Defendant-Husband's share at approximately $20,000.00; less than the $22,000.00 worth of corporate notes he had personally guaranteed. Therefore, the Trial Judge concluded that the defendant's value in the corporation was negative. On Appeal, the Appellate Court disagreed and remanded the issue for further consideration at the Trial Court level. The Appellate Division further stated:

> There are probably few assets whose valuation imposes as difficult, intricate and sophisticated a task as interests in a close corporation. They cannot be realistically valuated by a simplistic approach, which is based solely on book value, which fails to deal with the realities of the good will concept, which does not consider investment value of a business in terms of actual profit, and which does not deal with the question of discounting the value of a minority interest. Id. At 275. (Quoted in *Brown v. Brown* 328 N.J. Super. 466, 477 (App. Div. 2002), *certif. den.* 174 N.J. 193 (2002).

The Appellate Division further criticized Plaintiff-Wife's tactics throughout the litigation as she did not obtain expert assistance. An accounting expert experienced in the type of business involved here should have been produced by her to test Defendant's book value reliance and to assist the Court in applying the accounting and valuation principles appropriate in evaluating the specific business interests here. The Judge should not refrain from appointing his own expert as well, where the party's proofs do not provide him with sufficient foundation and guidance. In this context, it is appropriate, where circumstances warrant it, for the Judge to adapt the mechanism provided by the corporation act, for the valuation of shareholders' interest, by appointing an appraiser to make a non-binding report to it. *Id.* at 275.

The Appellate Division further directed the Trial Court as to how to apportion the value of the business:

> We point out that after the Judge determines the value of Defendant's interest in the corporation, he should then determine not only Plaintiff's distributable share thereof, but also the manner of her receipt of that share. The Judge will, of course, be free to direct, if necessary, to avoid a pyramid of the business itself, installment payments at such rates of interest and secured by such collateral as it deems appropriate. *Id.* at 276.

In *Balsamides v. Protameen Chemicals, Inc.*, 160 *N.J.* 352, 368 (1999), 734 A. 2d 721, 730, the New Jersey Supreme Court held:

> Experts exercise judgment at many stages in the valuation process. As a result, their credibility and reliability are critical. Only the Trial Court has the opportunity to see, hear and question the expert witnesses. Additionally, in complicated proceedings, such as this, the Trial Court's findings on valuation typically are only one aspect of the overall resolution of the matter. Appellate Courts should take care in accepting some and rejecting other findings of the Court, as they may disturb the logic and equitable balance of the Trial Court's other conclusions.

There is no single formula that will apply to each enterprise: each case presents a unique factual question, the solution to which is not within the ambit of any exact science. The reasonableness of any valuation depends upon the judgment and experience of the appraiser and the completeness of the information upon which his conclusions are based. *Bowen v. Bowen*, 96 *N.J.* 36, 43, (1984).

Most importantly, the process of business valuations is a fluid concept. The value of a business, at the commencement of divorce, may not be the same at the Trial or at settlement of divorce, as divorce actions may stay active with the Court for several years. For example, in *Goldman v. Goldman*, 275 *N.J.* Super., 452, 646, 2d 504 (App. Div. 1994), the Husband's car dealership had a significantly higher value at the time the Complaint was filed and had no value at the time of trial. Plaintiff-Husband poured approximately $400,000.00 of the parties' marital assets into the business in an attempt to save the business. Unfortunately, by the time of trial, the business had failed due to market fluctuations and not due to the bad faith of the Plaintiff-Husband. *Id.* at 458.

IF THEY HAVE ONE, YOU MUST HAVE ONE TOO.

As a general rule, when one side has an expert then, the other side should also have an expert. The only way you can avoid not having an expert is if you get in writing from your adversary stating the fact that he or she shall not be obtaining an expert. This can often lead the novice practitioner into the trap laid by the older attorney of providing the expert's name discovery and surprising you on the eve of discovery ending by providing a report which can leave you scrambling or calling your malpractice carrier. The best way to avoid this trap is to insist from your client, in the beginning, that if you think an expert is necessary that there be one retained right away. When you do things correctly you will not get into trouble. You can assure your client that the expense was well worth it when it comes to settlement or the time of trial when the judge has no option but to follow your expert's advice as to the value of the business obviously money well spent.

DOES YOUR CASE WARRANT THE FINANCIAL EXPENDITURE FOR AN EXPERT?

When the determination has been made by the attorney and the client that there is an asset which has to be valued your next question is: does this case warrant the financial expenditure for an expert. If the expert you want to utilize tells you that his or her retainer is ten or fifteen thousand dollars regardless of the size of the business, this expert must be evaluated very carefully. Not all businesses need the large firm, big retainer expert. The expert that is able to tell you, and the client, candidly whether there is the need to expend these type of fees in this case is the one you must choose. Then, once the initial evaluation is performed, the expert may need to do further work but you will know that the fees shall be necessary and your client will not have spent ten thousand to find out that the two man law firm just does not have any goodwill. You now have a very nice twenty-page report that tells your client that the value of the firm is the value of the used office furniture and equipment. Avoid this problem and retain the expert who can answer this question initially.

CAN YOUR EXPERT TESTIFY IN COURT?

Another question that must be asked of the expert is whether he or she has ever testified as an expert before. If they have not, you do not want to be the first. Find out by asking him/her the question right up front. If you fail to obtain the response to your question you may not like the look on your client's face when the trial judge does not let your expert testify. Usually, an excellent indication of your expert's ability to testify may be drawn from the initials on his or her letterhead. Is he or she a CPA, CFE, Cr.FA or a CVA? Is he or she a member of the American Board of Forensic Accountants or the American Institute of Certified Public Accountants just to name a few. Initials alone though, will not tell you if he or she has testified, so you must ask the question directly.

IS THIS THE CORRECT EXPERT FOR YOUR JUDGE?

Once you have determined if your expert has qualified to testify before, then the question you must ask is, is this the correct expert for your judge? The judge you have been assigned to may have a particular temperament such that, the most proficient technical expert, when on the stand, may just confuse or frustrate the judge. In a case such as this, you want to keep it simple, or the judge may just not understand the technical nuances and side with your adversary. This is a common mistake, where the attorney or the client fails to take into consideration the propensities of the judge who shall be making the decisions, and it can be a fatal one.

SHOULD THE PARTIES CHOOSE A JOINT EXPERT?

Many Judges want the parties and the attorneys to agree upon a joint expert. This may make sense in some cases. Obviously, there is a huge cost savings when your client only has to pay for one half of the expert. And obviously, the total overall fees shall be less. If the expert is truly independent, and can be trusted not to take extreme positions, then in that event a joint expert may be retained. You must however, as the professional, charged with protecting the interest of your client, have a very good handle upon the abilities, prior reports, and prior practices of the proposed joint expert. The expert may have certain predispositions as it comes to the valuation of a certain type of asset and you must be able to understand just where the expert is coming from. If the expert in valuing a business always uses a particular formula or cap rate which shall stick it to your client – you must know this in advance. As long as you are comfortable with the expert's abilities, and you have explained all of this to the client, a joint expert may be the way to go.

From a client perspective however, the retention of a joint expert may be a gamble. If for whatever reason the independent or joint expert begins to have more communications with the other side, or your client believes that the expert is somehow "siding" with the other side, your client may feel that they have become swayed by the other side or are working for the enemy. Once this impression has been formed in the minds of your client, it may be impossible for you to undue what has been done. When the final report is submitted your client may be looking at you as the professional to let the court know that the "joint expert" is really a shill for the other side. You will then have two problems on your hand, an angry client and an angry judge. The bottom line is choosing a "joint" expert carefully and make sure that you have confirmed your discussions with the client as to the retention of the joint expert carefully.

IS THIS THE CORRECT EXPERT FOR YOUR CLIENT?

You may have the right expert financially, from a credentials and testifying position and financially, but then you must determine if he or she is the right expert for your client. You must determine if your expert has the correct "bedside manner" for your client. If you have the client who is one who needs a lot of hand holding then in that event you must have an expert who is available to take time to help the client understand the issues. Also, you must choose the correct expert for the detailed and knowledgeable client. The client who has more than a general knowledge needs to know that your expert has a handle on all the issues. An expert who fails to instill confidence in the client will soon create a client who is going elsewhere.

CONCLUSION

It is critical that you have an expert who is the right expert. He or she must be able to testify, instill confidence in the client, and do the job effectively and cost efficiently. If you follow these guidelines you as the attorney will be very satisfied. More importantly, your client will be satisfied also.

CHAPTER 11

Litigating and Proving Child Support in High Asset or High Income Cases: What to do When a Heavy Hitter is at the Plate

Barry A. Kozyra and **Judith A. Hartz**

INTRODUCTION

High net-worth and high income individuals[1] ("Heavy Hitters") addressing child support[2] requirements and needs face a particularly daunting challenge in the presentation of proofs and what to expect in litigating the issue. Most attorneys and other professionals have limited experience in representing Heavy Hitters and even less in the context of developing an appropriate strategy in the emotional and complex context of a matrimonial proceeding which may also involve grounds for divorce, alimony, equitable distribution and child custody. Existing statutes, court rules and case law[3] do provide a skeleton for understanding the special challenges of those types of cases, but it is the creativity of counsel and other profes-

---

[1] For purposes of this discussion, high net-worth individuals are those having title to assets (exclusive of principal residence and retirement accounts) of $2,000,000.00, and high income individuals are those with net annual incomes from all sources in excess of $150,000.00 (above the New Jersey Child Support Guidelines). R 5:6-A. While these two numbers are to a degree arbitrary (some clients with lesser figures may be subject to the same analysis and some clients with greater, in rare circumstances, will not), they do provide a threshold for when Heavy Hitter treatment should be explored.

[2] While this discussion is limited to child support issues, special analysis must also be given to alimony and equitable distribution for the same individuals. However, as different statutory and case law considerations are employed in that analysis, both are beyond the scope of this review.

[3] See Section. I.

Barry A. Kozyra, Esq., is a partner at Kozyra & Hartz, LLC, Roseland, NJ.
Judith A. Hartz, Esq., is a partner at Kozyra & Hartz, LLC, Roseland, NJ.

sionals that is needed to develop the flesh necessary for obtaining a trier of fact's fair determination of child support.

LEGAL ANALYSIS

New Jersey recognizes that where a parent has the financial ability to provide for his or her child, the child is entitled to the benefit of the financial advantages available to that parent. New Jersey Courts have held that children are entitled to have their needs met consistent with the current standard of living of both parents, including a parent's good fortune. See *Connell v. Connell*, 313 N.J. Super. 426-430 (App. Div. 1998). Children are entitled not only to bare necessities, but the benefit of a parent's financial achievement. See *Dunne v. Dunne*, 209 N.J. Super. 559, 557 (App. Div. 1986). New Jersey has defined "high earners" as parents whose income far exceeds the norm, and whose wage levels substantially exceed the child support guidelines. See *Issacson v. Issacson*, 348 N.J. Super. 560, 565 (App. Div.) cert. den. 174 N.J. 364 (2002). High earners have also been defined as having the ability to "afford any rationally based award of child support." *Id*.

When determining a child's needs, courts must ordinarily look to the statutory criteria set forth in *N.J.S.A.* 2A:34-23(a), which provides as follows:

> In determining the amount to be paid by a parent for support of the child and the period during which the support is owed, the Court in those cases not governed by court rule shall consider, but not be limited to, the following factors:
>
> - Needs of the child;
> - Standards of living and economic circumstances of each parent;
> - All sources of income and assets of each parent;
> - Earning ability of each parent, including educational background, training, employment skills, work experience, custodial responsibility for children, including the costs of providing child care and the length of time and costs of each parent to obtain training or experience for appropriate employment;

- Need and capacity of the child for education, including higher education;
- Age and health of the child and each parent;
- Income, assets and earning ability of the child;
- Responsibility of the parents for the Court-ordered support of others;
- Reasonable debt and liabilities of each child and parent; and
- Any other factors the Court may deem relevant.

In circumstances involving "high earners" the maximum child support provided for in the New Jersey Child Support Guidelines should be "supplemented" by an additional award determined by application of the statutory factors in *N.J.S.A.* 2A:34-23(a).[4] See *Pascale v. Pascale*, 140 N.J. 583, 594-595 (1995).

In *Issacson v. Issacson*,[5] a case involving a post-judgment application for increased child support based upon the increased earnings of the payor's father from approximately $180,000 at the time of her divorce to over $500,000 per year and the maturation of the children, the court opined that:

> Determining a child's needs in these unusual financial circumstances presents unique problems. First, a balance must be struck between reasonable needs, which reflect lifestyle opportunities, while at the same time precluding an inappropriate windfall to the child, and even in some cases infringing on the legitimate right of either parent to determine the appropriate lifestyle of a child. This latter consideration involves a careful balancing of interests reflecting that a child's entitlement to share in a parent's good fortune does not deprive either parent of the right to participate in the development of an appropriate value system for a child. This is critical tension that may develop between competing

---
[4] The guidelines are not strictly applicable where family income exceeds the maximum tabled amount of $2,900 combined net weekly income. R. 5:6-A.
[5] Although Issacson involved a post-judgment application for modification of an initial child support award, its principles apply to all child support matters involving "high earners."

> parents. Ultimately, the needs of a child of such circumstances also call to the floor the best interests of the child. (Citations omitted.)
> *Issacson*, 348 N.J. Super. at. 582.

New Jersey Courts have also indicated that while a case may involve a high income earner who has the ability to pay any award that is reasonable and in the child's best interest, it does not mean that there should be an "exhaustive list" of items that must be paid by the high income earners. *Issacson* at 578.

> The promulgation of such 'needs' is not an open-ended opportunity for the parent to develop a 'wish-list' for a child that does not comport with the child's best interest: 'needs' is a relative factor in appropriate upbringing of a child and a reflection of the lifestyle of the parents. By way of example, the fact that a parent may be driving a luxury automobile does not mean that a child of driving age will be entitled to a similar luxury automobile, but the supporting parent's financial wherewithal may enable a child with a need for an automobile to enjoy the luxury of an automobile, suitable and appropriate for a teenager to drive and sufficient to meet the child's transportation needs. Judges must be vigilant in providing for "needs" consistent with lifestyle without overindulgence. As one court observed in dealing with high-income support, "practitioners dealing with situations such as this sometimes refer to the 'Three Pony Rule.'" That is no child, no matter how wealthy the parents, needs to be provided more than three ponies. Citations omitted.
> *Issacson*, 348 N.J. Super. at. 583.

Courts must render a child support award, mindful of established law stating that children of divorce have the right "to be supported at least according to the standard of living to which they have grown accustomed prior to the separation of their parents." See *Pascale v. Pascale*, 140 N.J. 583, 592 (1995) quoting *Guglielmo v. Guglielmo*, 253 N.J. Super. 531, 546 (App. Div.

1992). Such an award may include "bestowing benefits of nonessential items on the children to reflect such good fortune." *Loro v. Colliano*, 354 N.J. Super. 212, 223-24 (App. Div.) cert. denied 174 N.J. 544 (2002). This raises the question of the benefit to the custodial payee parent: it has been held that a court is not "offended" if there is some incidental benefit to the custodial parent from the child support payments, while "overreaching" in the name of benefiting a child is offensive. See *Issacson*, 348 N.J. Super. at 584.

PROVING THE CASE

Once an awareness of the current state of the law is acquired, a strategy must be developed and employed which puts the client's position before the trier of fact in the best light possible.[6] First consideration should be given to whether the case fits in the categorical definition of a "Heavy Hitter" and whether such a strategy needs to be employed at all.

Aside from borderline or marginal cases where application of the Heavy Hitter label is debatable, one (and sometimes both) of the parties can be reluctant to be viewed by anyone, including counsel, as a Heavy Hitter. At times, there is modesty or embarrassment about financial success or acquired wealth. At others there is suspicion or fear that the parties' resources will be unnecessarily exploited in the matrimonial process. These emotions and concerns are natural and are quickly recognized and dealt with by experienced counsel and professionals as early as the initial client conference or telephone contact.[7] The client must be given comfort that counsel is aware of the concerns and will guide them through the complex process as efficiently and painlessly as possible without unnecessary expenditures or sacrificing their principles or best interests. The reluctant Heavy Hitter, whether payor or payee, must be made to understand the need for accurate and complete disclosure of financial resources and the need to be responsive to the requirements of litigation. See *infra*.

---

[6] Child support issues are ordinarily decided by a judge. R. 5:6A. However, child support determinations can be referred by joint agreement to alternative dispute resolution, such as arbitration, or mediation. This discussion is limited to presentations before a trier of fact, whether judge or arbitrator (binding), as it assumes the parties would not be successful in mediation.

[7] Routine questions by counsel about economic resources are met with "why do you need to know that?" or vague estimates of income and ranges of values for property.

In contrast, some clients embrace the Heavy Hitter nom de plume and are almost willing to force themselves into the category even when their circumstances do not quite fit. This is more likely to be the case with payees than payors who want what they perceive as the benefit of such treatment. Experienced counsel and other professionals can quickly identify these clients, too. They are willing to boast, exaggerate and even fabricate economic circumstances in the hope that their anecdotes and estimates of assets and income or expenses will be accepted as true. They operate with the misguided conception that if they say everything is more, greater or bigger, the trier of fact will have to agree. Their views of appropriate child support may have no realistic proportion quantitatively or include qualitatively dramatic, expectations that cannot be met or achieved if a fair or reasonable outcome is expected. These clients must be cautioned to control their claims or demands as they risk being viewed as unreasonable or overreaching. The over the top Heavy Hitter, too, must be made to understand their own need to provide accurate and complete financial information.

The Rules of Court and discovery provide the needed tools for a start to the client's representation. A properly completed Case Information Statement ("CIS") gives basic information about financial circumstances involving income, expenses, assets and liabilities. $R.$ 5:5-2. Accompanying schedules may reveal the sources of income and its continuity or consistency. Disclosure is more limited when focusing on expenses. Similarly, limited detail – and virtually no corroboration – is provided when looking at assets and liabilities. Some Heavy Hitter payors are able to control "the quality and quantity" of disclosed financial information, thus presenting a reduced financial picture for the trier of fact.

But the Case Information Statement provides no more than a thumbnail sketch of what is needed for properly representing a Heavy Hitter payor or payee in a child support proceeding. In fact, it is virtually meaningless if considered alone as it provides insufficient detail for use before a trier of fact.

The Rules of Court allow for use of interrogatories, $R.$ 5:5-1(a), production of documents, $R.$ 5:5-1(d), requests for admissions, $R.$ 5:5-1(d), and depositions, $R.$ 5:5-1. When seeking information from a Heavy Hitter payor there will be a desire in answering to minimize the amount or breadth of responses about assets, income or expenditures. The payor's recollections will have faded as to values, amounts of money spent, events attended, items purchased and other indicia of wealth, whether by design or indifference.

In contrast the Heavy Hitter payee will attempt to provide "all" of the information that might exist (and more) as to the same assets, income or expenditures. Values and expenses will be remembered as higher, the quantity and quality of items purchased as greater and more expensive, whether by design or ignorance.

Either Heavy Hitter party seeking information must be thorough without being overbearing or obnoxious. Effort should be directed first at obtaining documentary proofs or corroboration. If the Heavy Hitter does not have the needed documentary proofs, counsel should try getting it from third parties, e.g. employers, accountants, vendors, taxing authorities, etc. Counsel for the Heavy Hitter must take care to be cooperative and responsive in answering discovery requests, as failure to do so will be viewed as obstreperous, counter-productive and warranting the award of counsel fees and costs to opposing counsel. If that occurs, it will be viewed as a victory by the adversary and a loss by the Heavy Hitter, whether actual or symbolic, decreasing the chance of a fair outcome whether by settlement or trial.

The Heavy Hitter payor should be using the same tools to inquire as to expenses for the child, something that has usually been ignored while the parties were a family unit. Given the Heavy Hitter's status, anticipated expenditures for the child will go beyond the norm of what is usually found on the CIS. For example, where music lessons are taught, it can be expected that the lessons will be individual, not group, the teacher a practicing professional, not someone supplementing income, the instrument owned and of fine quality, not a rented subpar instrument, etc. Needless to say, there can be vast qualitative and quantitative differences in answering these and other questions. Documentary proof should be requested of the payee by receipt, cancelled check, credit card statement, etc. Focus by the Heavy Hitter payor should be on expenses which go well beyond the norm. If music lessons are appropriate, does the child need a Stradivarius violin just because the Heavy Hitter can afford it? If fencing lessons are desired, should an Olympic coach be hired? Must the child's expenses include a chauffeur-driven limousine to music lessons – because the Heavy Hitter uses one?

Conflict is to be expected between payor and payee because the custodial parent will naturally share in some of the child's bounty. For example, if the child goes to a restaurant, takes a vacation and travels or attends an event, it may be anticipated that the custodial parent will accompany. Obviously, when considering a Heavy Hitter child's baseline for such expenses, the costs will often double and at a higher starting level than what might be considered "normal." Two airfares (first class?), two hotel rooms (deluxe?), etc. can add up very quickly – yet it is hardly likely that a trier of fact will deem same as unnecessary or extravagant if it reflects the past or current lifestyles of the child or payor. On the other hand, how many such vacations are needed or appropriate annually?

Use of other professionals should also be considered. Forensic or tax accountants may be needed to assist in ferreting out or analyzing assets and liabilities or income and expense information from a Heavy Hitter. If the economic circumstances of the parties are disparate, application may be made to have the Heavy Hitter pay for such expenses on an interim or final basis. *R.* 5:6A. In addition, these professionals may be particularly helpful in developing additional or parallel inquiries or sources for missing or supplemental documents. Alternatively, they may be needed by the Heavy Hitter payor or payee to explain the economic situation in the best light possible to the trier of fact.

Requests for admissions are an efficient opportunity to pin down the legitimacy of documents and the accurateness of select facts. As questions must be narrowly asked (as they will be broadly construed by the recipient), care must be taken in phrasing in order to avoid useless answers. Requests for admissions are effective (when enforced) because they can move a case in the discovery process (they must be answered within thirty days, or are deemed admitted), streamline proofs at trial, and force the adversary to be careful of positions taken (counsel fees can be awarded for improper answers).

Once the information gathering process is complete, depositions should be considered. Thought must again be given to the issue of who the Heavy Hitter is and how that relates to child support in the context of the state of the law.

Heavy Hitter payors are typically strong personalities: ambitious, hardworking, goal-oriented and successful. "Nothing but the best" or "money is no object" are frequent mottos when spending for themselves (and even others) if done at their choice. Accustomed to being in control of their day-to-day lives, as well as the lives of others, and often reigning over complex financial empires, they are ill-suited for being subjected to the control of the legal system and what seems to them as its inefficiencies. They chafe at the involvement of outside (or their own) attorneys and others in what they deem is private. Heavy Hitter payors want to end the process "now" on what they see as reasonable terms, without wasting time on what is not or should not be (in their view), in dispute. For example, they may question the need for filling out the CIS at all or completely answering written discovery, not recognizing the raised suspicion of the adversary and opposing party when answers are not fully supplied or the perceived "insult" to adversaries in not responding.

The Heavy Hitter payee is also a strong personality: the payee is accustomed to a luxury standard of living and what may be viewed as a pampered lifestyle. "Why should I accept less than what my child needs or wants?" and "what about the marital lifestyle we lived and how (s)he lives now?" captures the attitude of these parents. Often operating in the past when little or no limit on spending for their child or themselves had been acceptable, they see no reason to limit expenditures now. Consequently, they have difficulty seeing a way to end litigation by settlement if they believe it provides an avenue to obtaining the full amount of the child support they want. They often want to leave no stone unturned in their quest to find all income, expenses, debts and assets available "for the child."

The key element to succeeding at trial of almost any family law case is credibility. The party with the best perceived credibility can often do better before a trier of fact than one who has the best facts. So it is important to ask questions at trial that are fair and reasonable in tone and content and at the same time designed to portray the party as you may wish.

The following is a sample direct examination colloquy between counsel and a Heavy Hitter payor (former husband) involving a marriage with one child:[8]

    [After background questions as to residence, education, and employment]

    Q: Was there any discussion of children at the time of the marriage?

    A: Yes, (where appropriate) we had an agreement on children; it was

---

[8] In this example, a pre-marital agreement exists stating that the Heavy Hitter payor will pay any amount reasonable and necessary to provide for the child's needs.

in the premarital agreement. We had an agreement that she would not have a child until after the first year of the marriage.

Q: Why?

A: Because I wanted to give us some time to learn about each other living together.

Q: At the time, you were residing in _____?

A: Yes, I was.

Q: So (where appropriate) with regard to the specific items that are enumerated as your responsibility for any children born, you acknowledge that you are responsible without contribution from your ex-spouse; is that correct?

A: That is correct.

Q: As it relates to the items not covered for the care of your child beyond the scope of these specific items, what is your position?

A: That if she has any means, that she should make some contribution towards them.

Q: And are you willing to continue to abide by whatever is determined that you must pay as necessary to provide for your child's expenses?

A: Absolutely.

Q: (Where appropriate) You are presently following a court order to provide $_____ per month for your child's expenses and as child support; is that correct?

A: That is correct.

Q: And you are current on those payments?

A: Absolutely, every month.

Q: What is your position with regard to the amount of your present support payment of $_____ per month as being reasonable?

A: We've asked for a detailed figure on how it was being spent. I don't think we've ever gotten an answer, so at this time I would believe that $_____ for a _____-year-old child is more than adequate.

Q: Are you questioning your ex-wife's use of the child support throughout this litigation?

A: Yes.

Q: And what are you asking the Court to do with regard to any unaccounted for funds and her failure to account for proper use?

A: Put the money in a trust for my child.

Q: Are you willing to be bound by whatever the Court determines is reasonable and necessary for your child's support?

A: Yes.

Q: Now, Mr. Heavy Hitter, much has been made throughout these proceedings concerning a standard for determining child support, and the phrase "which shall be reflective of your overall economic circumstances at the time." Do you have any specific recollection of what was intended by that language or why it was inserted into the agreement?

A: The reason was to make sure that my child was as comfortable as possible knowing that I would probably have the resources to make him comfortable.

Q: Now, the child support statute that is in existence today requires a court to determine the standard of living of the parties. Was it your intention to go beyond the language of the statute in providing child support?

A: No, not really.

Q: Could you tell the Court what type of life-style you enjoy at the present time?

A: A good life style.

Q: Where do you reside?

A: I reside in Princeton, Boca Raton, and New York. I fly back and forth, sometimes by private jet, sometimes commercially. I take many vacations each year.

Q: What is your current income, sir?

A: About $__ million a year.

Q: And what is your net worth? I know you can't tell us to the penny, but your estimated net worth would be fine.

A: _____ million plus.

Q: Do you recall testifying in an earlier deposition that your income and your net worth was approximately $__ million and your net worth was $___ million?

A: Yes, I really do not pay that much attention to the numbers. So that might be correct.

Q: You testified that you have three residences. Do you have any servants at these residences?

A: Yes.

Q: And what type of staff do you maintain and where?

A: A housekeeping couple and a driver in New York. The couple sometimes travels with me to my other residence in Princeton, otherwise there is no staff there. I have one house person in Florida full time.

Q: What do they cost a year?

A: I think the couple are paid around $75,000 together which includes their benefits and a seasonal bonus. And if I remember correctly, about the same for the driver and half of that for the Florida servant.

Q: So to summarize your standard of living, what we've just covered essentially would lead one to conclude that you live a relatively high standard of living?

A: I also have a lot of expenses and liabilities. But it is a good life-style.

Q: But for purposes of child support, at the time this agreement was negotiated, was it intended that your child was to have servants and to fly around in private jets and to enjoy all of the luxuries that an adult would have?

A: As he grew older and if we were going someplace together, sure. So if I happened to be taking a private plane, he would be with me. But not all of the time.

Q: Well, let me ask you this question: If your ex-wife wanted to take your child on a vacation to Europe, is it your position that she should be entitled to fly with your child by private jet paid for by you?

A: No, not at all.

Q: Is it your position that she should have a driver and a staff associated with her residence?

A: I would think a nanny or housekeeper as I have proposed would be plenty.

Naturally, counsel for the Heavy Hitter will want to avoid reference to specific dollar amounts as much as possible. After all, what difference does it make? How many "ponies" need to be bought for a child, especially when the Heavy Hitter has offered to pay "whatever is ordered" that is reasonable? Needless to say, cross-examination will be used to demonstrate that anything is affordable.

Q: Okay. Now, what was your understanding of the language that the amount was to be reflective of your overall economic circumstances at the time?

A: Well, I am not an attorney, so I am really not the one that can define that. (Note: This is a particularly common, and bad, answer as it suggests that the Heavy Hitter has signed a document that he/she did not understand – a position that will be adopted and exploited by the adverse party when suitable including a challenge to the validity of the document itself.)

Q: I am asking about your understanding, sir.

A: My understanding of it is that my child would be taken care of in a manner that would suit him, where he didn't have to worry about his clothing or food or a home to live in or things of that nature.

Q: And did you expect he would have the opportunity to share in the increase of your income or net worth that you may have over the years?

A: He would be sharing in the increases as they affected me, especially if he was with me more often. If I had the opportunity to have him with me more often, he would be able to share that with me at all times.

Q: When you were living together as husband and wife and after your child was born, did you place any restrictions on where your ex-wife could shop for clothing?

A: She had a limit in how much she could spend, not where.

Q: What was the limit?

A: $_____ a month.

Q: So the $_____ a month was to include her expenses as well as the child's?

A: No; she had money of her own that I gave for her expenses. And if she needed extra money for my child, she would speak to me about it and I would reimburse her if I thought it was reasonable. And when she was living with me, if it was never more than another $_____ a month.

Q: Did you put any restrictions on her as to where she could shop for clothes for the child?

A: Not restrictions, but nothing that was spent was to be unreasonable. And when she was living with me, if it was never more than $_____. I mean, you know, I didn't want her to go out and buy a pony for a one-year-old.

Q: But she could shop at stores such as Saks Fifth Avenue, Bloomingdale's, Polo, Ralph Lauren?

A: Of course, absolutely, but those stores did not have a lot for my child.

Q: Now, the apartment in New York, do you rent or own it?

A: It's leased by one of my companies.

Q: And the rent is approximately $25,000 per month?

A: Well it is actually more, around $35,000 per month.

Q: Now you also indicated that you have an interest in a partnership that allows you use of a private airplane.

A: Yes, it is a Lear jet.

Q: And as part of that interest, you have the use of _____ hours of air time, correct?

A: That is correct.

Q: And when you do not fly with the private plane, do you fly first class?

A: Yes.

Q: Now, I also asked you questions during your deposition about charge cards and you indicated that your monthly bills were about $_____. Do you recall that?

A: I thought it was less, but maybe I said that, I am not sure.

Q: Do you own any motor vehicles yourself?

A: No, my company leases them for me.

Q: Do you have use of any vehicles?

A: Yes.

Q: You also have at your disposal a chauffeur-driven limousine?

A: That is correct.

Q: You indicated in another answer to a question that you spend three months of the year in each of your residences unless you're traveling, is that correct?

A: I said traveling or sometimes in the Hamptons.

Q: So would you say that of the 12 months of the year, you're vacationing three months?

A: Yes, or maybe four months.

Q: I think you indicated you have about 20 to 25 suits and you paid about $3,500 each for them. You don't have to worry about cleaning or alterations because that's included in the price.

A: That's correct.

Q: And you have your shirts custom made for you and they're about $200 or $300.

A: Yes, that is correct.

Q: And your shoes you buy off the rack, they're about $400 or $500.

A: Yes, really about $300 to $500, depending on what they are.

Q: Would you say that consistent with your life-style, then, that your child would be able to go on frequent vacations, as his school year allows, to the kinds of places you visit?

A: He can go with me all the time.

Q: Mr. Heavy Hitter, this year, did you take your ex-wife and your child on a vacation to _____?

A: Yes.

Q: Did you pay for it?

A: Yes.

Q: And did you go down by private jet?

A: Yes.

Q: And did you pay for their hotel room as well as a nanny?

A: Yes.

Q: Do you remember what the cost of that vacation was?

A: I think their rooms were $_____ a night each room.

Q: How many nights?

A: I think it was seven nights.

Q: Did that include food and things like that?

A: No.

Q: Who paid for the food and other things?

A: Who do you think? Me.

Q: Did you also pay for ground transportation back and forth from the airport?

A: Yes.

Q: And you have also indicated that when you are in New York and Florida, you usually go out for dinner four nights a week?

Litigating and Proving Child Support in High Asset or High Income Cases   157

A: Approximately.

Q: When your child's visiting with you and he gets up before you, who makes him breakfast?

A: The staff.

Q: Who gets him dressed?

A: The nanny.

In similar fashion, the Heavy Hitter's spouse should be carefully examined about her background and the financial circumstances of the child. The following is a cross-examination colloquy with the Heavy Hitter's ex-wife payee:

[After background questions as to residence, education, and employment]

Q: Since you last testified in depositions, I believe you got married, is that correct?

A: Correct.

Q: And since then, have you changed your residence?

A: Yes.

Q: Where are you living today?

A: Short Hills, New Jersey.

Q: Your child lives with you?

A: Yes.

Q: Who owns that residence?

A: My new husband.

Q: Can you describe the house for us?

A: It's on a wooded 1 acre lot. It has a living room, dining room, kitchen on the first level. You walk downstairs, to another level. My child has a play room there with his own bathroom. You walk down another level and there is another washroom and then a second playroom downstairs. There is a work room downstairs. From the main entrance you walk upstairs. My child has a bedroom on that level with his own bathroom. There is another bedroom for guests. Then the master bedroom suite is upstairs.

Q: Do you have any plans to move from that residence?
A: Not at this moment.

Q: Since you moved to that location, has your child changed schools?
A: No.

Q: How far is that from your last residence?
A: I would say approximately 3/4 mile.

Q: At present, are you contributing to the monthly expenses with respect to the residence?
A: No.

Q: Has Mr. Heavy Hitter continued to make all monthly payments to you pursuant to the premarital agreement, correct?
A: Yes.

Q: And he is current with respect to those payments?
A: I believe so, yes.

Q: He's never been even late with those payments, has he?
A: No, he has not.

Q: Please look at Exhibit No. 1, which is a Case Information Statement of yours. Can you tell us what that document is?
A: It is the Case Information Statement that my attorneys finalized.

Q: Did you participate in the preparation of this document?
A: Yes.

Q: If you would, on this particular document, would you turn to page 4? Do you have that in front of you?
A: Yes.

Q: My page 4 says "Monthly Statements, Part D" and starts with

"Shelter." Is that what yours says?

A: Yes.

Q: You have a rent figure there of $_____ per month. Do you see that number?

A: Yes.

Q: Where did you come up with that number?

A: I believe that we came up with that number — what it would cost to rent a house in the area of Short Hills, New Jersey.

Q: Who is "we"?

A: Myself and my child.

Q: You and your son came up with that number. That is what you're telling me?

JUDGE: He wants to know who put the numbers together.

A: I stated the accountant and myself.

Q: Just so it is clear, this number was selected by you and some accountant?

A: The number was selected by myself, the accountant and we contacted a real estate agent in the area to find out how much it would cost to rent a house.

Q: You never spent that kind of money for rent during the period of time that we're talking about?

A: No.

Q: You also have a utilities figure here of $ ____ a month. Do you see that number?

A: Yes.

Q: I take it you never spent that money for utilities, either?

A: No.

Q: This maintenance and repairs figure of $_____. What is that?

A: To the best of my recollection, I believe that is what was spent on maintenance and repairs.

Q: For what?

A: Well, when we moved into my previous residence with my family, my child did not have a room that was fitting of a baby. So I had to redo the room and paper it and buy furniture because Mr. Heavy Hitter wouldn't give me the crib, et cetera, for the child.

Q: Now there is no need to do that again because you already spent that money, correct?

A: There is no need to do what?

Q: Spend that $_____ to improve the room and get furniture for the child because you have furniture and you improved the room?

A: He has grown out of the room – crib. I renovated a second room at the other house for my child.

Q: You moved, correct?

A: Yes.

Q: You haven't bought new furniture since the latest move, right?

A: I did buy new furniture.

Q: For the move as well?

A: What do you mean, "for the move as well"?

Q: You said that included in this figure of $_____ a month was the fact you had to buy furniture for the child's room.

A: In the old room at my other residence, yes.

Q: That furniture you now have? You moved that furniture to your new residence?

A: No.

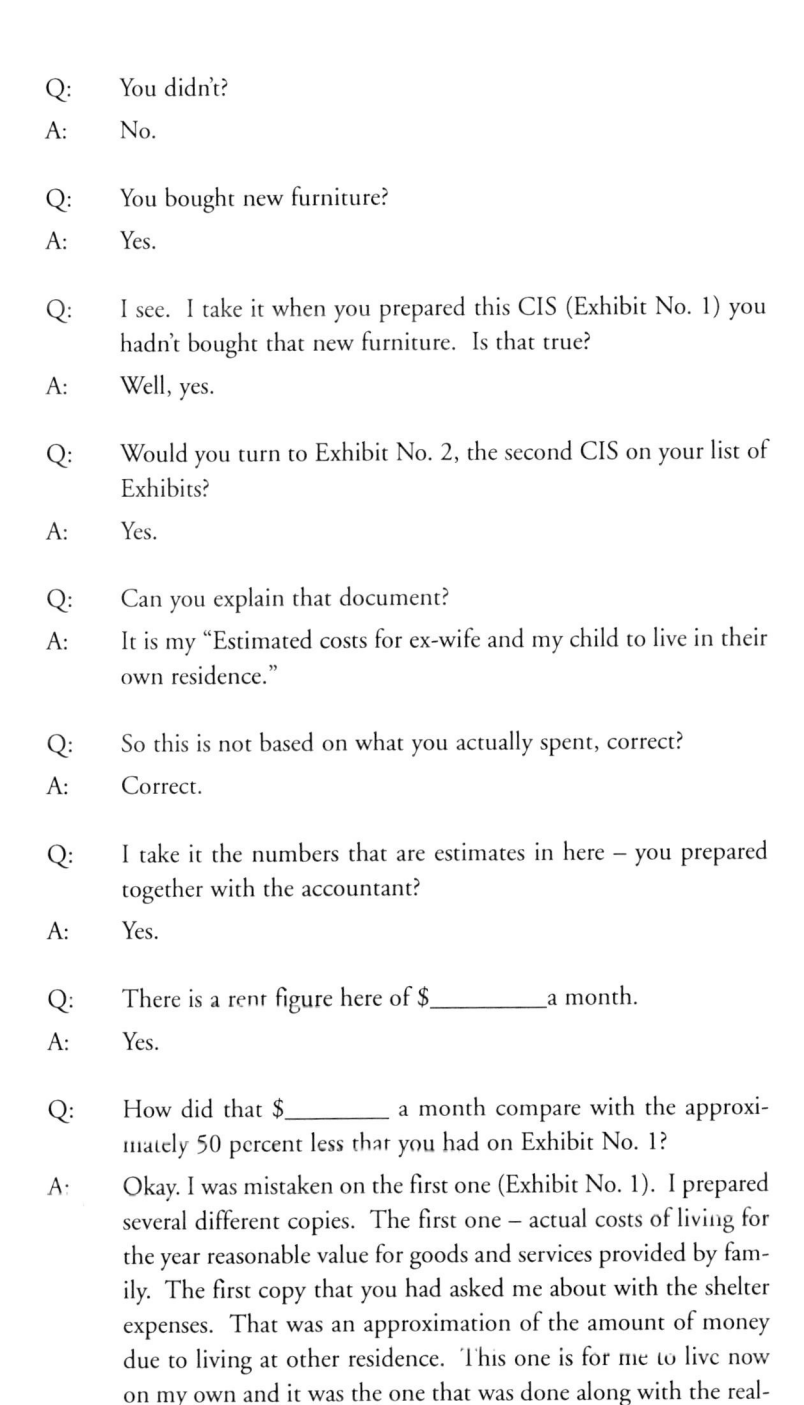

Litigating and Proving Child Support in High Asset or High Income Cases 161

Q: You didn't?
A: No.

Q: You bought new furniture?
A: Yes.

Q: I see. I take it when you prepared this CIS (Exhibit No. 1) you hadn't bought that new furniture. Is that true?
A: Well, yes.

Q: Would you turn to Exhibit No. 2, the second CIS on your list of Exhibits?
A: Yes.

Q: Can you explain that document?
A: It is my "Estimated costs for ex-wife and my child to live in their own residence."

Q: So this is not based on what you actually spent, correct?
A: Correct.

Q: I take it the numbers that are estimates in here – you prepared together with the accountant?
A: Yes.

Q: There is a rent figure here of $_____ a month.
A: Yes.

Q: How did that $_____ a month compare with the approximately 50 percent less that you had on Exhibit No. 1?
A: Okay. I was mistaken on the first one (Exhibit No. 1). I prepared several different copies. The first one – actual costs of living for the year reasonable value for goods and services provided by family. The first copy that you had asked me about with the shelter expenses. That was an approximation of the amount of money due to living at other residence. This one is for me to live now on my own and it was the one that was done along with the realtor and the accountant.

Q: Well, you didn't furnish any documentation for that first number, $_____ or whatever it was that you came up with, did you?

A: What do you mean by "furnish documents"?

Q: In showing your Case Information Statement, the first one, Exhibit No. 1, you came up with a number there. Now you're saying it was based on something else. Did you have any documentation to support that figure?

A: No. Because I could never afford to pay for any shelter with the amount of money that I was getting.

Q: I thought you just said that was the actual amount that would have been spent for shelter during that period of time on Exhibit No. 1.

A: I just said I didn't pay any money out for any kind of shelter..

Q: Where did the number come from?

A: That is what it would cost living at my family's house.

Q: Do you have any documentation to support that?

A: What? Living with my family?

Q: That it would cost that much money, yes.

A: Just what my family was paying for their mortgage.

Q: Do you have any documentation to show that?

A: The accountant had the documentation.

Q: From your family?

A: He contacted my family and he asked for numbers.

Q: No. I didn't ask whether he contacted your family. I'm trying to understand if there is some document for me to look at to see how you arrived at the number. Did you have a document?

A: No, I didn't have a document.

Q: This $_____ number that you also put on here for mortgage and taxes; there is no documentation to support that number, is there?

A: Just what the accountant and the realtor had put together.

Q: I'm asking you if there is documentation to support the number. Are you aware of any?

A: I believe there was a letter by the realtor to the accountant.

Q: So that is the only documentation that you would say supports that number?

A: Yes.

Q: If you would now turn to Exhibit No. 3. That's the third Case Information Statement you provided. If you look at the first page, at the top of it, it says "Actual Costs for Calendar Year 2003." Correct?

A: Yes.

Q: Did you participate in the preparation of this document?

A: Yes.

Q: And this one actually represents what you spent in the year 2003, correct?

A: Yes.

Q: If you would turn to page 4 you have three expenses listed. They are the same storage expense, the same maintenance and repair expense. Now you've added a telephone expense, correct?

A: Of some $667 month.

Q: That is a telephone for you and your child?

A: It is my cell phone and the house phone, yes.

Q: Does the child have a cell phone?

A: Yes.

Q: He does. Does he have his own number?
A: Yes.

Q: How old is he now?
A: _____ years old. We just purchased it for him.

Q: If you would turn now to Exhibit No. 4 and tell me when you have that in front of you.
A: Yes.

Q: Now, on this particular exhibit you have listed your child's monthly expenses at $14,900.00, correct?
A: Yes.

Q: Mr. Heavy Hitter currently pays you $_____ a month in support, correct?
A: Yes.

Q: And he's been paying that for some period of time. Correct?
A: For about _____ years, I believe.

Q: I'm going to ask you about some of the items that you have listed here, particularly the ones that show up in the child's expense column. Starting at the top, we have "Storage and Moving Expenses" of $_____ a month. Correct?
A: Yes.

Q: I take it that is for lockers that you were renting, correct?
A: Correct.

Q: Now you only have one of those, correct?
A: Correct.

Q: And the other one is going to be emptied shortly, I presume, too?
A: At some point, yes.

Q: When?
A: I don't have an exact date.

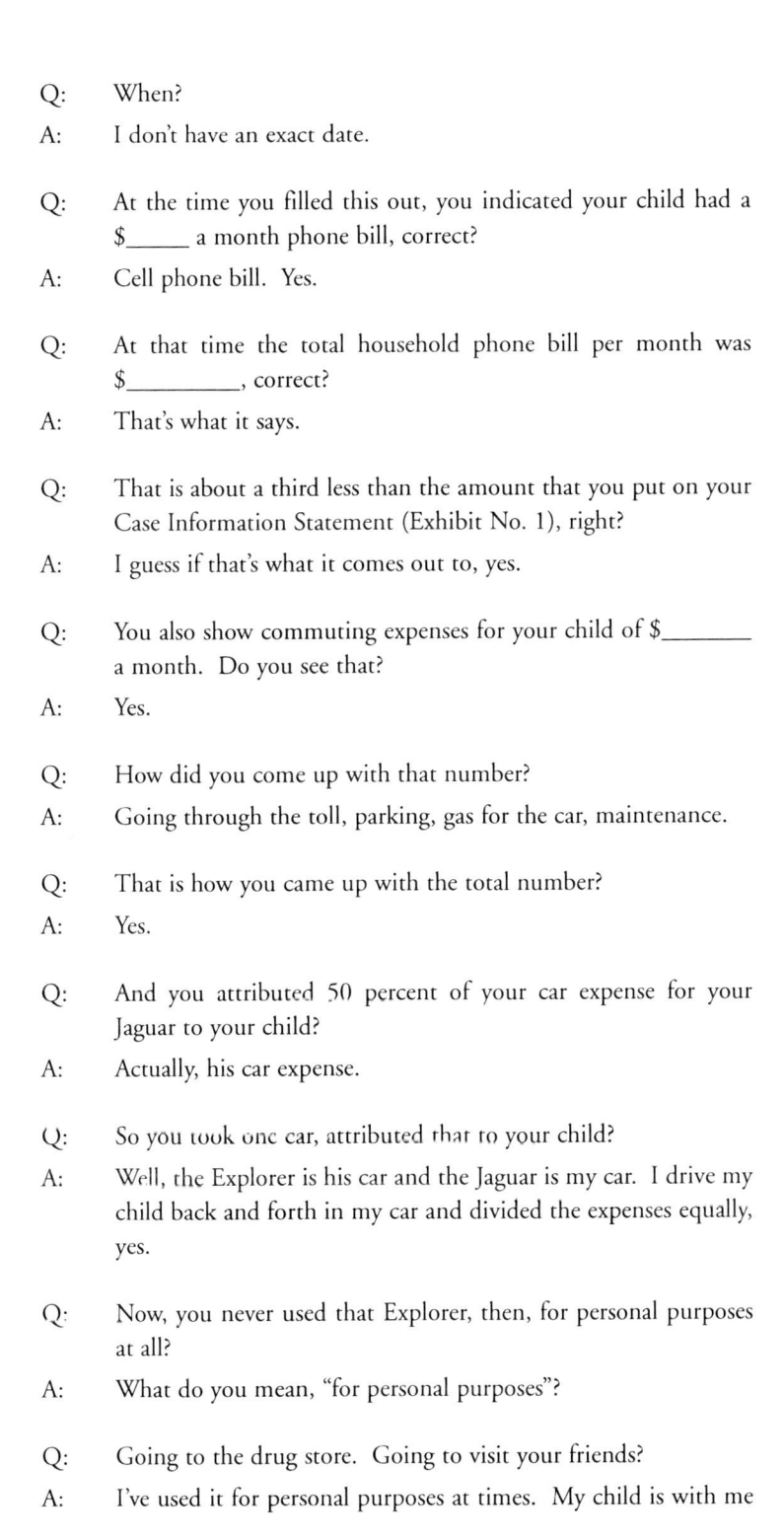

Q: At the time you filled this out, you indicated your child had a $_____ a month phone bill, correct?
A: Cell phone bill. Yes.

Q: At that time the total household phone bill per month was $_____, correct?
A: That's what it says.

Q: That is about a third less than the amount that you put on your Case Information Statement (Exhibit No. 1), right?
A: I guess if that's what it comes out to, yes.

Q: You also show commuting expenses for your child of $_____ a month. Do you see that?
A: Yes.

Q: How did you come up with that number?
A: Going through the toll, parking, gas for the car, maintenance.

Q: That is how you came up with the total number?
A: Yes.

Q: And you attributed 50 percent of your car expense for your Jaguar to your child?
A: Actually, his car expense.

Q: So you took one car, attributed that to your child?
A: Well, the Explorer is his car and the Jaguar is my car. I drive my child back and forth in my car and divided the expenses equally, yes.

Q: Now, you never used that Explorer, then, for personal purposes at all?
A: What do you mean, "for personal purposes"?

Q: Going to the drug store. Going to visit your friends?
A: I've used it for personal purposes at times. My child is with me

most of the time, you know.

Q: You took 50 percent of auto expenses and said that is your child's, correct?

A: I also took 50 percent and put it towards me. I thought that was fair, since the expenses are the majority on the Explorer.

Q: Essentially, you have two vehicles, right?
A: Yes.

Q: You combined the expenses for the two vehicles, right?
A: Yes.

Q: Divided it in half?
A: Yes.

Q: And said "one is for him and one is for me"?
A: What do you mean?

Q: Half is for him and half for me?
A: Yes, in effect, the expenses are about the same for both cars. I use the Explorer more than I use the Jaguar.

Q: You would say the expenses for the Explorer for your child are more; is that what you're saying?
A: I would say so. I probably use the Explorer 90 percent of the time.

Q: You're the sole driver of each of these vehicles?
A: At this time, yes.

Q: In adding these expenses that you come up with here, you have "food" and "home." You divide the monthly expenses. Half is for him and half is for you?
A: Yes.

Q: I think you indicated that with respect to restaurants you divided that up by a different percentage. Is that correct? That was

Litigating and Proving Child Support in High Asset or High Income Cases   167

        actually 60/40, is that true?

A: I don't recall the exact amount attributed to myself because of the times that I had gone out, myself, without my child.

Q: You also have a line down there for domestic help, correct?

A: Correct.

Q: Do you have domestic help?

A: In this past period of time I did.

Q: From the period of time January of _____ to May 31st _____ you had domestic help?

A: Yes.

Q: Who was that?

A: I had somebody come in on a part-time basis while my family was away as they would normally do the washing, cleaning the house.

Q: You attributed half of that expense to your child?

A: Yes.

Q: Is there any documentary evidence of that expense?

A: No, I paid cash.

Q: Now I'll move down the list to a couple of other expenses you have on here. You have "MYLAWYER#1". Do you see that particular line item?

A: Yes.

Q: You attributed to your child ½ of your legal fees from Mr. MYLAWYER#1 – who was your prior divorce counsel, correct?

A: Correct.

Q: You attributed to your child $7,500.00 a month of MYLAWYER#1's bills?

A: Correct.

Q: Of course, you don't have MYLAWYER#1's as counsel any longer, is that correct?
A: Yes.

Q: You have other counsel to succeed him?
A: Yes.

Q: You also have down there "MYCHILD'S LAWYER and expenses," which I presume is Mr. MYCHILD'S LAWYER is that correct.
A: Yes.

Q: You have $2,500 a month for Mr. MYCHILD'S LAWYER?
A: Correct.

Q: That is 100 percent of Mr. MYCHILD'S LAWYER bills, is that correct?
A: Yes.

Q: As your child's responsibility?
A: Yes.

Q: You also have down "Maintenance and Repairs" again. Do you see that item?
A: Yes.

Q: That you have down as $_____ a month, right?
A: Yes.

Q: That looks to be something like two-thirds of the expenses for that particular line item, correct?
A: About that.

Q: Let me take you back to Exhibit No. 3 for a moment. I was asking you about a maintenance and repair expense that you listed for your child at $_____ a month, which is almost five times higher than you have in your Case Information Statement,

Exhibit No. 1. Can you explain why?

A: Because his room was redone.

Q: So once the room is redone, you wouldn't have that expense each month, correct?

A: Correct.

Q: So I take it the amount was higher that month because, perhaps, that was the month that the bills came in? Is that why it would be that high?

A: Well, some of the months. I mean, this was a period from January through May. So, yes.

Q: All right. Now, supposing this case ends, which it will?

A: You think?

Q: You would agree you would have no more monthly expense of Mr. MYLAWYER#1 of $7,500 a month, correct?

A: I really can't answer that. I thought seven years ago I wouldn't have this expense.

Q: When the case is over, you wouldn't have attorneys' fees of that amount. Would you agree?

A: I would hope so.

Q: The same would be true of Mr. MYCHILD'S LAWYER? He would be done?

A: Mr. MYCHILD'S LAWYER would be done.

Q. Those two numbers, right there added together, is some $10,000 a month?

A: Right. If that's what it comes out.

Q: That is simple math. We can add those together and it is exactly $10,000 a month, true?

A: Yes.

Q: If you subtracted those legal fees from the total child support for the monthly period, which is some $14,894.79, you would agree, I take it, that the number would come out to $4,894.79, correct?

A: You're asking did the two numbers that you're talking about add up to that amount and you're deducting it from the $14,000 plus figure?

Q: Yes.

A: That is what it comes out to be.

Q: The monthly expense for your child, aside for attorneys' fees, from January through May 31st of ____ is something less than $5,000 a month. Correct?

A: I don't understand what you're asking me.

Q: I said your monthly expenses for your child that you report here on this schedule, once you subtract attorneys' fees, are something less than $5,000 a month, correct?

A: If you take your scenario, yes.

Q: Obviously, there are other expenses in here that would be reduced by reason of the fact that you moved into a new residence, correct?

A: Yes. Reduced and increased. There are things on here that I was unable to purchase for my child because I only get $7,000 a month now.

Q: I understand you're getting $7,000 a month. But when you take out the attorneys' fees, you only have $5,000 a month in expenses, right?

A: If you go by this schedule, yes.

Q: And it is your schedule, right?

A: Yes.

Q: In this schedule you also have included payment for private school, correct?

A: Yes.

Litigating and Proving Child Support in High Asset or High Income Cases 171

Q: In fact, Mr. Heavy Hitter is responsible for and has offered to pay 100 percent of your child's education expenses, correct?

A: On top of this?

Q: No.

A: I don't understand the question.

Q: But isn't it a fact that Mr. Heavy Hitter has offered on numerous occasions to pay for that expense above your $7,000? He's offered to pay for that 100 percent as required by the premarital agreement?

A: I didn't understand it as that.

Q: You have forgotten the testimony that you have given in this proceeding in which I showed you various correspondences to your counsel in which Mr. Heavy Hitter has said he will pay 100 percent of those expenses. Do you recall seeing those?

A: Well, I'm unclear as to how Mr. Heavy Hitter was going to pay it. Whether it was going to be out of the child support payment, he was just going to deduct it or over and above. Secondly, when it came to this, under the prenuptial agreement he's supposed to be paying it directly to me. Since I paid for my child's schooling since he was a year and a half old even when Mr. Heavy Hitter wasn't paying child support, I just continued in that manner.

Q: Mr. Heavy Hitter offered to pay 100 percent of the child's school, correct?

A: This is just recently, if you are putting it in those terms, yes.

Q: When you say "just recently," isn't it a fact that he offered to do that two years ago?

A: Just when we started coming to arbitration he offered to do that. Yes.

Q: No. Isn't it a fact that he offered to pay last year for your child's entire educational costs?

A: He said he wanted to pay for his schooling.

Q: And he offered to pay for 100 percent of it?

A: I was actually kind of confused. That is why this never had taken place. Because Mr. Heavy Hitter, on one hand, was saying I was getting too much in child support and yet he wanted to give me more money. So —

Q: He offered to pay, consistent with the premarital agreement, for 100 percent of your child's education costs, did he not?

A: Yes, he did.

Q: Does the Agreement say he's supposed to pay for school directly to you and not to the school?

A: That was my understanding. I mean, he allowed it to happen that way all these years.

Q: Isn't it a fact that Mr. Heavy Hitter offered to pay the school expense all of last year and, in fact, he offered to pay it retroactively? Isn't that true?

A: I didn't understand that.

Q: You didn't read the letters that your lawyers sent to you?

A: I didn't understand it to be that. I had spoken to Mr. Heavy Hitter directly about it.

Q: So you would agree, then, if Mr. Heavy Hitter would be paying the education expense – that is, the child's private school that you listed here – and you were paying that directly, that the $_____ a month I mentioned to you earlier would be reduced by that amount in actual expenses for your child, correct?

A: Going by this sheet, yes.

Q: These are numbers that you provided?

A: Yes.

Q: And I haven't even begun to address the maintenance and repairs number that you have down there, which is for decorating, I believe you said, of some $_____ a month, correct?

A: Yes.

Q: If we subtracted that expense, you'd be down to $_____ a

Litigating and Proving Child Support in High Asset or High Income Cases   173

        month, correct?

A: By your numbers, yes.

Q: They're really your numbers, aren't they?

A: If you are deducting away, that is the number it comes up to.

Counsel for the Heavy Hitter payee might consider redirect examination as follows:

REDIRECT

Q: Mr. Heavy Hitter's attorney's questions of you concerning the Case Information Statements, particularly Exhibits No. 1, No. 2, and No. 3. There were some questions about expenses being lower in last year than in the year back. Do you recall those questions?

A: Yes.

Q: Could you please explain to the Court why your child's expenses were lower in _____ than they were in _____?

A: Well, one of the reasons – Mr. Heavy Hitter had taken us all on vacation for my child's springtime vacation, which, normally, I would have to bear all that expense through child support, and he had paid for that. So that lowered it. Also, the expenses decreased because I just didn't have the funds because now I was paying more to my attorneys and the accountants. So that decreased the amount of moneys that I had available to spend on my child.

Q: You were still receiving from Mr. Heavy Hitter $_____ a month?

A: Yes.

Q: What were you spending that $_____ per month on?

A: The majority of it goes to attorney fees.

Q: Do you still owe Mr. MYLAWYER#1's firm any money?

A: Yes, I do.

Q: Approximately how much?

A: I believe it is somewhere around $_____.

Q: Do you still owe the forensic accountant that was assisting you in the preparation for this case any money?

A: Yes.

Q: How much?

A: I owe him, I believe, somewhere between $20,000 and $25,000.

Q: Do you still owe the firm of MYLAWYER#2 money?

A: Yes, I do.

Q: Approximately how much?

A: I believe it is somewhere — I don't know. Around $_____. Something like that.

Q: Do you still owe MYCHILD'S LAWYER money?

A: Yes, I do.

Q: So, again, the $10,000 a month you are receiving from Mr. Heavy Hitter is being used for what purpose?

A: Well, for attorneys and accountants. I mean, my average bill, I think, for my attorney fees from the beginning of this case was anywhere between $9,000 a month, to sometimes $15,000 a month just for my own personal attorneys' fees.

Q: With the available money that you have been receiving for child support, have you been able to provide the lifestyle for your child, consistent with that which you had when you were married with Mr. Heavy Hitter and had your child?

A: Not even close.

Q: Could you explain why not?

A: Because I don't have the funds. I mean, I receive $_____ a month, which none goes to housing since I live with my family because I can't afford housing, or I couldn't before I remarried. I couldn't afford a nanny. I couldn't take him on vacations or buy

Litigating and Proving Child Support in High Asset or High Income Cases 175

or do the things for the child, that I would have been able to do while we were married.

Q: Such as?

A: Such as every year we rented a yacht at Christmas and went down to the Islands for a good month, month and a half. I would never be able to even — never mind rent the yacht, but pay a bill for a month and a half, a month or whatever, to take the child. There were times where we've gone away on vacation. We can't even afford to fly First Class just because the funds aren't there or stay in the places that we would have stayed when I was married.

Q: Do you currently have availability to a private aircraft for travel?

A: No, I don't.

Q: Or a helicopter for travel?

A: No, I don't.

Q: Or a chauffeur-driven limousine for travel with your child?

A: No.

Q: Do you have any estimate of what it has cost you for this litigation throughout the years it has been ongoing?

A: I think I probably paid over a million dollars.

If counsel for the Heavy Hitter payor believes the lifestyle has been understated, recross-examination can be expected:

Q: With respect to your lifestyle, since your separation from Mr. Heavy Hitter, have you been to France?

A: Yes.

Q: One time or more than once?

A: I've been there twice. My child has been there once with me.

Q: How about Hawaii?

A: My new husband took us to Hawaii.

Q: You went with your child, correct?
A: He paid for my child.

Q: So he is paying for your child's expenses now?
A: He's paying for all the housing because I don't have enough money at this point.

Q: How about the cruises that you have been on? How many cruises have you been on?
A: I believe my child and I went on three or four.

Q: So the vacation expenses that you have shown on your Case Information Statements that you have for your child – you haven't had to pay those expenses?
A: Well, the Hawaii trip and some of the Florida trips don't show up in the vacation expense because my new husband had to pick up the tab for that. Mr. Heavy Hitter paid for the trip to San Juan. He was willing. I thought it was very nice. If we went to San Juan, he would pay for me and my child to go there.

Q: How about the cruises? Were they paid for?
A: I used to save up my frequent flyer credits. Every year I'd have all those credits and use them to take my child away.

Q: So there hasn't been any expense for those trips?
A: No. The expense doesn't show up. That means my expenses are actually lower than they would be.

Q: You were directed with respect to these issues to prepare an accounting with respect to child support in this matter?
A: Well, Mr. Heavy Hitter's attorneys requested it. He was saying I wasn't spending it on the child. So he actually requested it.

Q: But there were Courts that ordered that, is that correct?
A: Yes, they did.

Q: Did you ever prepare such an accounting to explain what you did with your child's money?
A: Yes. On several occasions including this one.

Q: What is the accounting that you have that you tell me that you prepared pursuant to the Court Order?

A: We came to this hearing. This is it. Whatever my accountants prepared.

Q: You have requested a clothing expense for your child of $1,200 a month?

A: Yes.

JUDGE: How many days a week does your child wear jeans?
THE WITNESS: Does he wear jeans?

JUDGE: Yes.
THE WITNESS: He never wears jeans.

JUDGE: Chinos?
THE WITNESS: He has a school uniform this year. When he's not in school he likes to wear the surfing pants that zip off.

JUDGE: Do you know the cost of those pants are what?
THE WITNESS: I don't even know. I don't even pay attention when I shop.

Q: I don't think they're $1,000 a month, are they?
A: Correct.

Depending on the parties' relationship and the needs or demands of payee and payor, the questions should develop along the lines of the parties' experiences. The answers given should be informative without exaggeration by either party.

CONCLUSION

Representation of a Heavy Hitter in the child support context requires a considered understanding of the law, the client and lifestyles of payor, payee and child. Limited income and modest asset cases require cautious balancing so as to allow all to live reasonably afterward. Heavy Hitter cases demand a different approach so as to comply with the law's general guidelines and avoid payment of far too much – or too little – in child support.

Preparation for hearing using the rules of discovery and development of a strategy designed to provide a comfortable lifestyle for the child without excess should be the goal of either the Heavy Hitter payor or payee. Counsel should prepare the client for that approach emotionally and through presentation of proof before the trier of fact. Asking for too much or offering too little in child support will put the litigants in the hands of a trier of fact who will view extreme behavior as not credible, which can lead to an unbalanced award of child support.

CHAPTER 12

Do Court Preferences Exist in Cases of Matrimonial Dissolution Involving the Valuation of Closely Held Companies?

James A. DiGabriele and **Gabriela V. Simoes**

INTRODUCTION

Divorce court usually has relatively little to do with the dissolution of a once happy relationship. Instead, it is the principal arena for the often acrimonious process of allocating a couple's accumulated wealth and some of their future earnings. The value of a closely held company can be a significant part of the total accumulated wealth of a marital estate. As a result, business valuations play an increasingly crucial role in the divorce settlement process. In divorce action, the value of a small business is often estimated in absence of actual sale. As a result of the difficulties inherent in the estimation process, this chapter analyzes preferences of the matrimonial court relating to valuation of closely held companies.

REVIEW OF THE LITERATURE

The issue of valuation is a continuing one since it resides at the heart of many financial controversies. Valuation of securities of a closely held company, for which there is no ready market, is particularly challenging (Bajaj, David, Ferris and Atula. 2001). Business valuations play an increasingly crucial role in the divorce settlement process. For starters, the data retrieval process may lack volunteered cooperation. This adds an additional dimen-

---

James A. DiGabriele, CPA, CFE, CFSA, DABFA, MSM, MST, Cr.FA, CVA, Partner/Managing Director of DiGabriele, McNulty & Co. LLC, West Orange, NJ.

Gabriela V. Simoes, Lucent Technologies, Murray Hill, New Jersey.

sion to the valuation process in a matrimonial setting, in that the chosen methodology of the valuation analysts must be explainable to the court regardless of the obstructions (Cenker and Monastra, 1991).

Equitably apportioning a couple's assets would be a complex task in the best of circumstances, but the intense emotions of divorce increase the complexity by an order of magnitude (Scott, 1995). Unfortunately, a few judges are not comfortable with accounting fundamentals, which allows them to be misled into what has come to be called "multi-dipping" valuations (Scott, 1995).

In divorce action, the value of a small business is often estimated in absence of actual sale, as a component of an overall division of marital assets. The business may have goodwill evidenced by "excess" cash flows (Aalberts, Clauretie and Matoney, 2000).

"Excess" cash flows are those greater than could be expected from tangible assets alone. In many cases "excess" cash flows of the business may be due to unique human capital of its owner/manager (Aalberts, Clauretie and Matoney, 2000).

In such cases, actual sale would likely require covenant-not-to-compete as evidence of this human capital. Misclassification of "excess" cash flows into goodwill causes a portion of value of human capital of one spouse to be transferred to the other. Generally, courts have determined that value of covenant-not-to-compete is separate property, and goodwill is community property (Aalberts, Clauretie and Matoney, 2000).

A valuation for divorce purposes is measured against a class of buyers in the same status as the present owner, not a hypothetical investor. By contrast, a valuation for estate tax purposes must take into consideration diminished earning capacity due to the loss of a key person and is measured against a hypothetical control investor (Zipp, 1992). The valuation procedures in divorce valuations are the same as are used in willing-buyer purchases. However, all the adjustments necessary for the willing-buyer valuation may not be appropriate for the divorce valuation, so the resulting value in divorce valuation may be different (Zipp, 1992).

WHY THE DIVORCE VALUATION IS DIFFERENT

The following characteristics identify substantive differences between a divorce valuation and a closely held company with a willing buyer:

1. State law defines marital property subject to valuation and distribution, whether or not the same property could be sold to a willing buyer at any price (Zipp, 1992).

2. The business is not being sold and the only willing buyer is the current owner. Thus, the appraisal's objective is to determine the value to the current owner in the marital community (Zipp, 1992).

3. The basis of value is determined differently for a sale, and risks associated with a management change are not relevant. Also of interest to the willing buyer but not to the divorce court is the business's value when combined with the buyer's existing enterprise for economies of scale or special benefits from items such as patents, copyrights or management personnel (Zipp, 1992).

4. Not all business assets are valued for a sale, but all may be marital property. In setting a price for the sale of a closely held business, an owner ordinarily excludes certain assets from the valuation. For example, cash and cash equivalents, such as marketable securities owned by the business, generally are not sold. Neither are nonoperating assets, such as investments in partnerships, art objects and raw land. These assets and related liabilities usually are retained by the owner and, hence, excluded from a willing-buyer valuation. Divorce valuations include all business assets, whether or not they might be sold to a third party in a hypothetical sale (Zipp, 1992).

5. Goodwill value presumes continuation of the business and is predicated on future earnings. However, most state marital property laws exclude post divorce income from equitable distribution, and divorce value may not consider future earnings. Hence, while the willing buyer values the business with reference to future earnings, the divorce value doesn't consider post divorce efforts and earnings (Zipp, 1992).

Further, the divorce court is concerned with the business's value in the present owner's hands as a marital asset subject to equitable distribution statutes and monetary awards. Equity between the parties does not generally influence the willing buyer's valuation perspective (Zipp, 1992).

Most states require divorce courts to value marital property as of the divorce date. Certain property, such as that acquired before the marriage or after the divorce, is excluded (Zipp, 1992). In making a business valuation for divorce purposes, it is critical to include only property considered marital by state law. In particular, intangible assets that depend on future efforts and continued operations after the divorce are not considered in a divorce valuation (Zipp, 1992).

Additional Valuation Issues in Matrimonial Divorce

Mastracchio and Mastracchio (1996) address the issue of the value of an education or license acquired during a marriage. While marriage is not usually perceived as an economic partnership, if a divorce is involved the concept becomes paramount. One of the most difficult issues to resolve is the equitable financial arrangements when one spouse has sacrificed education, career, and standard of living to enhance the earning capacity of the other spouse. Most states do not recognize enhanced earning capacity as a marital asset.

Luttrell and Freeman (2001) add to the controversy that has been turned upside down in the Tax Court; the tax effecting of an S Corporation's income stream in the valuation process.

According to Luttrell and Freeman (2001), S corporations are often undervalued in the context of marital dissolutions. This is a result of business appraisers who incorrectly reduce earnings for hypothetical income taxes in the valuation of these entities. This adjustment is often mired in complex spreadsheets and calculations, and can be difficult to spot. Take heed, however, because this erroneous adjustment can result in an understatement of value of 30 to 40 percent.

Luttrell and Freeman (2001) review several theories advanced by valuation analysts to support the imputation of entity-level income taxes where none are actually incurred:

Theory	Arguments Advanced by Valuation Analysts
Potential buyers are C Corporations	The pool of potential buyers are C Corporations who pay Corporate income tax.
Required rate of return is derived from C corporations earnings after corporate income tax.	The empirical sources used to develop the capitalization rate are based on corporate.
S corporation status	A corporation can lose its tax exempt status by violating certain rules set forth in the Internal Revenue Code.
Phantom income	An owner recognizes taxable income from an investment without an equal receipt of cash flow.
No deferral of individual income tax	The nature of pass through entities such that taxable income is immediately recognized by the owners on their individual income tax returns.
Difficult to raise capital or sell stock	There are limitations on what type of entities can own stock in an S Corporation and how many shareholders can exist
Other disadvantages of S corporations are best accounted for by inputting C corporation taxes	Since it is difficult to quantify the impact of certain S corporation limitations on a company, one must simply assume the company is a regular corporation and apply full corporate income tax rates.

Evans (1994), reviews business valuation theory and case law in matrimonial divorce to show that the courts emphasize how non-fictional factors must be considered for a thorough valuation. State law and court cases determine the presence or absence of goodwill, and sometimes suggest how to quantify it. This is especially important in the valuation of professional practices. The controversy over goodwill in an equitable distribution begins with the fact that income attributable to post-divorce activities is not subject to equitable distribution. Goodwill, however, is a going concern concept, since its value is predicated upon the future earnings of the business. One theory holds that since the earnings generated by the goodwill are received after the divorce, goodwill is not a marital asset. The opposing point of view counters that future earnings to be received after the divorce would not be possible without the presence of goodwill at the time of the divorce. The issue of personal (professional) goodwill versus business (commercial or practice) goodwill should be addressed by the valuation analyst because the courts recognize this distinction, particularly in professional practices. Personal goodwill is associated primarily with the individual and his or her knowledge or skills. These traits are not considered to be transferable or saleable. Business goodwill, on the other hand, is tied to the name, reputation, location, facilities and staff of the business separate from its owner. Business goodwill is transferable, and assumes that customers, patients or clients would continue to patronize that business regardless of ownership.

A well-established valuation concept is that the value of any enterprise rests upon the net current value of its tangible assets and its ability (or lack thereof) to generate excess earnings, over and above fair compensation to any owner-employee(s) for work performed, and over and above a fair return on the current value of such tangible assets. Appraisals of ongoing enterprises invariably consider both factors. Net current value of tangible assets sets the lower limit on valuation, and the goodwill value, if any, when added to the net current value of tangible assets, defines the upper end of the valuation range. Goodwill value is based entirely upon the amount of residual profit, if any; the business can generate annually (Zipp, 1992).

In terms of dividing everything fairly – tangible assets, practice value and future income. For a professional practice these elements overlap; they are facets of the same income stream. When the practice is valued improperly, by including an amount for personal services (future pretax income) which may or may not be part of a possible future sale transaction, the result – at best – is to award the same dollars to the spouse more than once i.e. a "multi dipping" valuation (Zipp, 1992).

SUMMARY

The valuation of closely held companies is more of an art than a science with valuation standards that vary. Several organizations; the American Society of Appraisers (ASA), the Institute of Business Appraisers (IBA), and the National Association of Certified Valuation Analysts (NACVA) have each developed and issued a comprehensive set of business valuation standards (Cercone, 2002). In addition, numerous IRS pronouncements and publications also provide professional guidance with regard to valuation methodologies, procedures, data sources, and reporting (Reilly, 2003). However, these organizations and the Internal Revenue Service have not been able to curb the controversy of valuation in the matrimonial dissolution process.

As a result of the complications surrounding the matrimonial dissolution process, the question arises of whether or not the valuation process has been streamlined by the courts. In particular we ask;

1. In matrimonial court, is gender preference in the valuation of closely held companies related to industry, jurisdiction and valuation approach?
2. In matrimonial court, is there a valuation approach preference?

Method

Description of Sample Formation

The Business Valuation Library Data Base was used to search for matrimonial dissolution cases for the most recent six (6) to ten (10) year period that included the following components:

1. Decision in favor of the husband or wife's valuation expert.
2. Valuation approach presented and valuation approach preferred.
3. Type of closely held company being valued and respective industry.
4. Jurisdiction.

Table 1 illustrates the steps in the data extraction process.

Table 1.
Description of Sample Formation

	Cases
(1) Matrimonial valuation cases identified in the database.	50
(2) All facilities in (1) excluding those limited to non-duplicate cases	33
(3) All facilities in (2) excluding those where gender, valuation approach, industry and jurisdiction could not be extracted.	26

Fifty (50) was the selected sample used in this study. Used as the breaking point, this amount initially appeared to be enough data to provide an unbiased sample. The data extracted from the matrimonial court cases ultimately tested were: gender, valuation approach presented and preferred, type of closely held companies being valued, and jurisdiction. These variables were used to address the aforementioned research questions.

Binary logistic regression (BLR) was selected as the testing process for the first question. The dependent variable (gender) was coded as a dummy variable (0,1). The independent variables were industry and jurisdiction. The model was interpreted using the Percent Correct Predictions (PCP) statistic and χ^2 goodness-of-fit test (Chi-Square Test). The PCP statistic assumes that if the percent is greater than or equal to .50 then the event is expected to occur, or not to occur, otherwise. This statistic is further interpreted as follows; the greater the Percent Correct Predictions, the more likely the tested relationship will yield the expected outcome. The Chi-Square statistic was also used to determine if the overall model was statistically significant. The results are illustrated in table 3 and 3a.

For question number 2, a goodness-of-fit test was performed to determine if the income, asset, and market-based approach were equally likely to occur (after removing those cases in which a combination of approach was employed). The chi square goodness-of-fit test determines if the observed frequencies are different from what we would expect to otherwise find. The results are illustrated in Table 4.

Results

Descriptive Statistics

A total of 33 court cases were included in the present analysis. Initially, descriptive statistics were computed for each of the four study variables: gender preference, industry, jurisdiction, and preferred valuation approach. The 33 cases involved 17 different industries; therefore, only the most common industries (business services and health services) were included in subsequent analyses. The remaining industries comprised a category labeled "other." Similarly, the 33 cases involved 18 different jurisdictions, therefore, only those that included the location of at least three cases (Ohio and Wisconsin), were included in subsequent analysis. The remaining jurisdictions comprised a category labeled "other." Table 2 below presents the frequencies and percentages based on the 33 cases.

Table 2
Descriptive Statistics

	Frequency	Percentage
Gender Preference		
Male	10	30.3
Female	16	48.5
Both / Neither	7	21.2
Industry		
Business Services	5	15.2
Health Services	5	15.2
Other	23	69.7
Jurisdiction		
Ohio	4	12.1
Wisconsin	3	9.1
Other	26	78.8
Valuation Method		
Income	16	48.5
Asset	6	18.2
Market	3	9.1
Combination	8	24.2

Inferential Statistics

To address the first research question, gender preferences were examined using a Binary Logistic Regression (BLR), with gender preference as the dependent variable and industry, jurisdiction, and valuation approach as the independent variables. Given that 7 of the 33 cases involved no gender preference, the test was conducted without those cases as a result of the nature of the dependent variable. The model was interpreted using the Percent Correct Predictions (PCP) statistic and a χ^2 goodness-of-fit test (Chi-Square Test). The PCP statistic assumes that if the percent is greater than or equal to .50 then the event is expected to occur, or not to occur, otherwise. This statistic is further interpreted as follows; the greater the Percent Correct Predictions, the more likely the tested relationship will yield the expected outcome. The Chi-Square statistic was also used to determine if the overall model was statistically significant.

The BLR yielded a result of 65.40%. The model therefore predicts that 65.40% of the time, family court will be gender biased when also considering industry and jurisdiction, if the case involves the valuation of a closely held company. Table 2 illustrates that court decisions in favor of females represented 48.50%, and court decisions in favor of males represented 30.30%. Consequently, a fair conclusion based on the interpretation of these results is that family court will be bias toward females 65.40% of the time, when the marital dissolution case includes the proper valuation of a closely held company. These results are illustrated in table 3 below:

Table 3
Inferential Statistics

	Classification Table for Gender The Cut Value is .50			
	Predicted			Percent Correct
Observed	0	1	Total	
0	3	7	% 30.00	
1	2	14	% 87.50	
Overall Percentage	% 19.20	% 80.80		% 65.40

Chi-Square Test for Overall Model

In addition to the PCP statistic, the Chi-Square statistic was also used to determine if the overall model was statistically significant. The result was statistically significant (χ^2 (2) = 11.461, p = .120). See Table 3a. below.

Table 3a.
Model Fitting Information

Chi Square	11.461
df	7
Sig.	.120

Chi-Square Test Frequencies

In order to address the second research question, a χ^2 goodness-of-fit test was performed to determine if the income, asset, and market-based approach were equally likely to occur (after removing those cases in which a combination of approach was employed). The result was statistically significant (χ^2 (2) = 11.120, p = .004). Examining the frequencies in Table 2 indicates that income-based approaches were used more often than the asset-based or market-based approach.

Table 4.
Chi-Square Test Frequencies

Test Statistics	Observed N	Expected N	Residual
Income	16	8.3	7.7
Asset	6	8.3	-2.3
Market	3	8.3	-5.3
Total	25		
Chi-Square[a]	11.12		
df	2		

DISCUSSION

In the case of marital dissolution, the valuation of securities of a closely held company is predominantly challenging. There has been a valiant attempt to develop guidelines for the process of accurately allocating a value to an enterprise. The result of the inability to curtail the storm of controversy present within the matrimonial divorce procedure emphatically yields the particular question of whether or not the court system has streamlined the valuation process. In matrimonial court, the question of gender preference in the valuation of closely held companies related to industry, jurisdiction and valuation approach has yielded an inferential test result ascertaining that family court will be bias, siding with females more than 50 percent of the time. This model also proved to be statistically significant. Furthermore, the Chi-Squared Test resulted in unequally distributed valuation approach preference by family court, confirming court preference of the income-based model to the asset-based and market-based model.

Earlier research has unearthed various previously disregarded components that are now realized to be an essential part of the equitable valuation of closely held companies for the purpose of marital dissolution. Such issues include intangible assets contingent on the continuation and future of the organization, goodwill, enhanced earning capacity, and undervaluing or overvaluing because of incorrect earnings reduction based on hypothetical income taxes. The complexity of properly valuing an entity for the purpose of marital dissolution emphasizes the necessity for a well-informed family court that can offer an unbiased and evenhanded assignment of the value of a closely held company.

Results of the sample formation confirmed that court preferences do in fact exist in matrimonial cases involving the valuation of closely held companies. Courts reveal gender preference, exhibiting a larger than 50 percent chance of favoring the wife's expert over the husband's expert. Courts further reveal preference when it comes to the approach utilized to value the closely held company; the income approach is preferred over the market and asset approach. Due to the sensitivity and uniqueness of each marital dissolution case, the presence of court preferences can only be detrimental to the valuation of the organization resulting in an inequitable apportionment of a couple's assets.

The research compiled thus far yielding the aforementioned results span a time line of approximately 6 to 10 years. Future research, extending a sample numerous years, would capture interesting results, illustrating trends that have evolved over time in the court system. While it is our conclusion that court preferences regarding gender and valuation approach do exist, the formation of such a trend, and when it may have flip flopped from one gender to the other, or one approach to other would also paint a telling picture. Furthermore, increasing the variables that are tested gives rise to interesting questions as well. Upon case-by-case research, extracting information such as certification criteria for the expert analysts involved in the valuation could further prove or even disprove the theory of courtside manipulation. The center stage issue would then be a correlation between the credentials, certification, and expertise of expert analysts; whether based on such credentials; expert analysts are predominately bias towards a particular valuation approach. However, this pilot study tends to statistically express the existence of court preferences in matrimonial dissolution cases involving the valuation of closely held companies.

REFERENCES

Aalberts, Robert J., Terrence M. Clauretie, and Joseph P. Matoney. "Small Business Valuation: Goodwill and Covenants-Not-to-Compete in Community Property Divorce Actions." *Journal of Forensic Economics* 13 (2000).

Atula, et al. "Firm Value and Marketability Discounts." *Journal of Corporation Law* 27 (2001).

Cenker, William, and Carl Monastra. "Business Valuations: Constraints Imposed by Divorce." *Journal of Legal Economics* 1 (1991): 7-21.

Cenker, William, and Carl Monastra. "Business Valuations: Constraints Imposed by Divorce." *Journal of Legal Economics* 1 (1991): 7-21.

Cercone JR., Louis J. "Uniform Standards for Business Valuations." *The CPA Journal* 72 (2002).

Evans, Frank C. "Business Valuation: Equitable Distribution in Divorce." *Pennsylvania CPA Journal* 65 (1994).

Freeman, Jeff W., and Mark S. Luttrell. "Taxes and Undervaluation of 'S' Corporations. (Marital Dissolutions)." *American Journal of Family Law* 15 (2001): 301-306.

Mastracchio, James N., and Nicholas J. Mastracchio Jr... "Professional License Value in a Divorce." *The CPA Journal* 66 (1996).

Mastracchio, James N. "Professional License Value in a Divorce." (n.d.).

Reilly, Robert. "Professional Guidance on Valuation from IRS Publications." *Valuation Strategies* 6 (2003).

Scott Jr., Robert B. "Determining the Value of a Small Business for Divorce Proceedings." *The National Public Accountant* 40 (1995).

"Small Business Valuation: Goodwill and Covenants-Not-to-." (n.d.).

Zipp, Alan S. "Business Valuation for Divorce." *Journal of Accountancy* 173 (1992).

CONTRIBUTING AUTHORS

Richard A. Campanella, CPA, is Partner and Director of Accounting & Due Diligence Services for DiGabriele, McNulty & Co., LLC, West Orange, NJ.

James A. DiGabriele, CPA, CFE, CFSA, DABFA, MSM, MST, Cr.FA, CVA, is Partner/Managing Director of DiGabriele, McNulty & Co., LLC, West Orange, NJ, an accounting firm specializing in forensic/investigative accounting and litigation support. Certificates: Certified Public Accountant, licensed in the State of New Jersey, a Certified Fraud Examiner, Certified Financial Services Auditor, Certified Forensic Accountant, and Certified Valuation Analyst. Degrees: Master of Science in Taxation from Seton Hall University and Master of Science, Management/Finance from New Jersey Institute of Technology. Currently in the process of completing a Doctor of Professional Studies degree with concentrations in Economics and Management from the Lubin School of Business at Pace University in New York.

Judith A. Hartz, Esq., is a partner at Kozyra & Hartz, LLC, Roseland, NJ. Ms. Hartz has engaged in the general practice of law with a primary focus on civil litigation and a specialty in family law (adoption, custody and visitation, domestic violence and divorce), contracts, medical malpractice, criminal defense, and wills, trusts and estates. She is a member of the New Jersey State Bar Association (Family Law Section) and the Essex County Bar Association (Member of the Family Law Executive Committee), and is a former Trustee of the Essex County Bar Association. Ms. Hartz has also participated in the Family Law Inns of Court.

David C. Hesser, is an attorney at Gold, Weems, Bruser, Sues & Rundell, in Alexandria, LA, and is a Certified Divorce Financial Analyst. He received his Juris Doctor from the University of Arkansas, William H. Bowen School of Law, his L.LM. from Tulane University Law School, and is currently enrolled in a part-time Ph.D. program through the University of Leicester, England, researching collaborative divorce. He is a member of the Collaborative Professionals Group of Louisiana and has served on the Rules/Membership Committee. He has lectured and assisted in collaborative divorce seminars including: Collaborative Divorce Training, Loyola University Law School, 2004, and Collaborative Divorce Seminar Panel Discussion on Mental Illness: Expanding the Framework for Developing a Cultural Competent

Community, Louisiana College, 2003. He filed Louisiana's first successful collaborative divorce case in 2003.

Mark Kohn, CPA, CFE, CVA, ABV, is a forensic accountant specializing in marital dissolution litigation in the Los Angeles area. His practice consists primarily in the areas of business valuations, the determination of gross income available for support, and searching for hidden assets.

Barry A. Kozyra, Esq., is a partner at Kozyra & Hartz, LLC, Roseland, NJ. Mr. Kozyra is admitted to the bars in New Jersey and New York, the Third Circuit Court of Appeals, and the United States Supreme Court. He has handled federal and state litigation at both the trial and appellate levels. Mr. Kozyra has been responsible for litigation in the areas of contract, commercial law, corporation and partnership law, criminal defense, professional licensing (legal, medical, pharmaceutical and others), attorney ethics, family law (divorce, custody and adoption), insurance, environmental protection, malpractice (legal, accounting and medical), real estate, condominium law, constitutional law, bailment, employment and torts. Mr. Kozyra is a member of the American Bar Association, the New Jersey State Bar Association, and the Essex County Bar Association (Chairman of the Criminal Law Section, 1988-1989). Mr. Kozyra is a recipient of the New Jersey State Bar Association's Service to the Bar Award.

Alison C. Leslie, is associated with the firm, Cutler, Simeone, Townsend, Tomaio & Newmark. Admitted to both the New Jersey and New York bars, Ms. Leslie has devoted her practice exclusively to family law and matrimonial related matters.

Joseph M. Lo Campo, Seton Hall University, South Orange, NJ. He was graduated with high honors Magna Cum Laude in Business Administration, with the concentration in Accounting from Seton Hall University. He is currently a candidate for the Master of Science degree in Public Accounting at Seton Hall University.

Dr. Susan M. Mangiero, is a managing member of BVA, LLC, a business valuation and litigation support company. She has over fifteen years of experience in the areas of valuation and risk assessment. She has written for publications such as *RISK*, *Valuation Strategies*, *Expert Evidence Report*, newsletter for the Institute of Internal Auditors, and *Investment Lawyer*. She is author of the recent book, *Risk Management for Pensions, Endowments, and Foundations* (John Wiley & Sons, Inc., 2005).

Contributing Authors

James F. McNulty, CPA, CFSA, DABFA, Cr. FA, is partner with DiGabriele, McNulty & Co., LLC, Certified Public Accountants, Clark and West Orange, NJ. Mr. McNulty is a former IRS Auditor and Revenue Agent. Mr. McNulty has broad experience with a wide variety of matrimonial valuation matters.

William J. Morrison, CPA/ABV, president of Morrison & Company. He is a CPA licensed in New Jersey and Florida and has over 25 years of experience as an investigator and accountant. Mr. Morrison is Accredited in Business Valuation (ABV) and is a Diplomate of the American Board of Forensic Accounting (DABFA). Prior to founding Morrison & Company, he served as a Special Agent for the Federal Bureau of Investigation, an internal auditor, and a Certified Public Accountant. He has served as an expert for the Superior Court and the Supreme Court of New Jersey.

Thomas J. Reck, CPA/ABV, is a licensed CPA in New Jersey and is Accredited in Business Valuation (ABV). He has 14 years experience in public accounting in industries including: retailing, legal services, medical and dental services, publishing, real estate management, condominium associations, trucking, wasteflow and not-for-profit organizations. Mr. Reck is skilled in all aspects of forensic accounting, including business valuations, audits, compilations, reviews, and tax and cash flow analyses.

Bruce L. Richman, CPA/ABV, CVA, CDP, is Managing Director, Business Valuation and Divorce Consulting Services, Trenwith Valuation, LLC, an affiliate company of BDO Seidman, LLP, Chicago, IL.

Gabriela V. Simoes is a Financial Analyst for Lucent Technologies and a member of the corporation's Financial Leadership Development Program. She was graduated Summa Cum Laude in Business Administration, with the concentration in Finance, from Seton Hall University. She is currently a candidate for the Master of Science degree in Management, with the concentration in Finance, at Babson College.

Joyce C. Somerville, CPA, is a manager of the Matrimonial Group at RosenfarbWinters, LLC in Tinton Falls, NJ. She is a licensed CPA in New Jersey and New York. Ms. Somerville is a member of the New Jersey Society of Certified Public Accountants and serves as Co-Chairman of the Monmouth/Ocean County Litigation Services Committee. In addition, she is a member of the American Institute of Certified Public Accountants. Ms. Somerville has lectured on several occasions on matrimonial accounting issues for the New Jersey Society of CPAs.

Paul Townsend, Esq., is partner with Cutler, Simeone, Townsend, Tomaio & Newmark, LLC, Morristown, NJ.

Lili A. Vasileff is a Certified Financial Planner™ professional and co-president of the Association for Divorce Financial Planners. She has conducted numerous public seminars on the topics of divorce financial planning and investments as keynote speaker and workshop leader for local, regional and national groups. She has been quoted in *Smart Money* magazine, *Working Mother* magazine, the *Wall Street Journal*, *New York Times* Sunday Business Section, *Morningstar*'s article series on "How to be an Expert Witness," the *Journal of Financial Planning*, and the *Financial Times* U.S. edition.

Kevin R. Yeanoplos, CPA/ABV, ASA, is the Managing Member of Yeanoplos Drysdale Group, PLLC, a firm with offices in Tucson, AZ and Salt Lake City, UT, that specializes in the areas of business valuation, financial analysis and litigation support. Mr. Yeanoplos has extensive experience, having valued over 750 businesses for a variety of purposes, including divorce, gift and estate taxes, mergers and acquisitions, ESOP's, and other litigation. He has valued a broad spectrum of companies in various industries, including aircraft parts manufacturers, construction companies, automobile dealerships, restaurants, and various retailers. He has also valued various professional practices, including accounting firms, law firms, and medical and dental practices. Mr. Yeanoplos has evaluated economic loss suffered by parties in cases involving contract disputes, medical malpractice and wrongful termination.

INDEX

A

alimony 2-6, 17-24, 31, 35, 72, 95, 134, 141

American Institute of Certified Public Accountants (AICPA) 26-28, 138

appraiser 33, 37, 39, 41-42, 124, 135-136, 182, 185

B

business valuation 31, 109, 133-139, 179, 182, 185, 191-192

C

Case Information Statement (CIS) 2-4, 146-149, 158, 161-165, 168, 173, 176

cash flow method 35-39, 58, 114, 180, 183

Certified Divorce Financial Analyst (CDFA) 19, 23, 28

Certified Financial Planner (CFP) 23, 27

Certified Public Accountant (CPA) 23, 26-27, 71, 138

child support 2-3, 5, 6, 17-20, 24, 31, 35, 72, 103-106, 110, 141-178

collaborative divorce 19-30

co-mingling 66, 106-107

common sizing 122

community property 65, 67, 69, 180

D

deferred compensation 17, 33, 37-38, 92, 123

deposition(s) 2, 7, 50-51, 62, 111, 115-116, 123, 146, 148, 152, 155, 157

direct examination colloquy 149

discovery 2, 6, 17, 22, 37, 72, 109, 111, 113, 115-116, 122, 129, 131, 134, 137, 146-149, 178

disposable income method 2, 5-6, 12-15

dissipation 18, 68, 101, 102, 114

double dipping 35, 44

E

equitable distribution 1, 5-6, 18, 65, 67, 69, 100, 108, 133, 141, 181, 184

excess earnings method (EEM) 35, 43-44, 48, 184

expenditure method 62

expert witness 1, 133, 136

F

fair market value 33, 35, 43, 61, 124

family law 20, 22, 43, 50, 109, 149

forensic accountant 1-4, 49-53, 63, 66-81, 84-91, 101-102, 104-108, 110, 116, 133-134, 138, 174

formula method 43-46, 48

fringe benefits 9, 71, 73, 75, 77, 79, 81, 83, 85, 87, 89, 91-93, 95

G

gift(s) 9, 54, 60, 63, 66, 69, 94, 98-99, 114, 116-117, 124, 128

goodwill 33, 41, 44, 46, 135, 137, 180-181, 183-184, 190

H

heavy hitter 141, 145-153, 156-158, 160, 164, 171-178

hidden assets 11, 49, 51, 53, 55, 57, 59, 61, 63, 113

hidden income 4, 10, 71
See also hidden property, unreported income

hidden property *See* hidden assests

homemaker contribution 101-103

I

industry ratio(s) 59

inspection (of physical premises) 74, 83-84, 109, 115, 121, 123

Institute for Divorce Financial Analysts 23, 28

interviews and interviewing *See* oral inquiry

J

joint experts 138-139

Judgment for Dissolution 99

L

lifestyle method 2-4, 6, 8-10, 17, 37, 54-58, 63, 115

M

marital assets *See* marital property

marital property 24, 39, 65-69, 97-108, 133, 136, 180-182

mediation 20-21, 29, 145

N

net worth method 60, 62-63, 133-114

neutral financial professional (NFP) 19, 21-30

no-fault divorce 19

normalizing (of financial statements) 109, 111

O

oral inquiry 3-4, 74-84, 87, 90, 93, 111, 115, 121, 130

P

Pendente Lite 2, 6, 17

perquisites 3-4, 9, 33, 36, 71-73, 91, 95
See also fringe benefits

phantom income 9, 183

post-nuptial agreement 98, 103

pre-nuptial agreement 41, 98

private investigator(s) 56, 59-60, 63

property distribution(s) 18, 65, 68, 71, 104-105, 124

Q

Qualified Domestic Relations Order 1, 20, 107

R

related party transactions 109, 124

retirement benefits 20, 69, 92, 108
See also deferred compensation

retirement investments 107 *See also* deferred compensation

S

site visit *See* inspection

subpoena 50, 52, 54-57, 61, 111, 118, 123, 129

sufficient competent evidence 73

T

tax consequences 5, 7, 17-18, 20, 24, 40, 68, 105

transferred property 11

transmutation 107

treasury method 43 *See also* excess earnings method

U

unreported income 3-4, 10, 49-51, 53-63, 83, 93, 114, 120, 130 *See also* hidden income

Printed in the United States
112978LV00002B/366/A